CW00518014

ENLIGHTENED BUSINESS

Leadership for Sustainable Success

◇◇◇◇◇◇◇◇◇◇◇◇◇◇◇◇◇◇

JOOLZ LEWIS

Josie,

keep shining and sharing your wisdom,

With Love,

Joolz

*Enlightened Business
Leadership for Sustainable Success* © Joolz Lewis

ISBN 978-1-909116-34-4
eISBN 978-1-909116-35-1

Published in 2014 by SRA Books

Design concept and cover design by Oro Design

The right of Joolz Lewis to be identified as the author
of this work has been asserted by her in accordance with the
Copyright, Designs and Patents Act 1988.

A CIP record of this book is available from the British Library.

All rights reserved. No part of this book may be reproduced, stored
in a retrieval system, or transmitted in any form or by any means,
electronic, mechanical, photocopying, recording or otherwise,
without the prior written permission of the copyright holder.

No responsibility for loss occasioned to any person acting or
refraining from action as a result of any material in this publication
can be accepted by the author or publisher.

Printed in the UK by TJ International, Padstow

TO AMMA

My teacher and guiding light;
for showing me the path to Love.
Words, for so long my currency in this world,
fail to express the depth of my gratitude.

TO MARCUS

For keeping my feet on the ground
while giving me space to fly.

& TO ALL YOU BUSINESS WARRIORS

Who take daily steps towards your own
version of enlightened business.

WHAT PEOPLE HAVE SAID ABOUT ENLIGHTENED BUSINESS

"The call went out for more inspirational leadership. Joolz has heard that call and most importantly she has been responsive and this book is her response. In *Enlightened Business*, Joolz inspires you to a whole new possibility of the purpose of your work and leadership. Read, be inspired, and come home to the heart of you." *Nick Williams, author of eight books including* The Work We Were Born To Do.

"Do you want to find a way to be both spiritual and effective as a leader? This book gives you one idea per chapter theme which is tested and practical. Pick the ideas that you need right now and try them. Uncover and utilize your authentic presence and highest potential to make a difference in your life, your organization and in the world." *Cindy Wigglesworth, author of best-selling book* SQ21: The Twenty-One Skills of Spiritual Intelligence

"The energy and creativity that derives from that state of consciousness that is greater than one's habitual self has always been said to be 'ineffable'. It is an experience that cannot be spoken about; as it says in the Tao and religions it can't be explained in logical linguistic linear ways. Joolz Lewis has connected these wisdoms into a useful, clearly articulated manual to help business people, leaders and managers of large organisations to tap into that experience and enable them to invest that energy into their organisation and people to develop entities that will succeed and grow for the good.

If I'd had this leadership book during my time at M&S it would have given me the confidence to lead more from my intuition and with faith in my 'purpose', and my leadership would have looked very different." *Lord Andrew Stone, former Joint Managing Director of M&S*

CONTENTS

FOREWORD

There's an old movie called *Field of Dreams* about an Iowa farmer, Ray Kinsella, who hears a voice from his cornfield say to him, 'If you build it, he will come.' Ray interprets this message as an instruction to build a baseball field on his farm, believing that if he does, Shoeless Joe Jackson will be able to come and play baseball again. Shoeless Joe was a member of the infamous Black Sox team, a team believed to have intentionally lost the World Series in 1919. The Black Sox team was banned for life from playing baseball. Ray has support from his family, but the townsfolk think he's crazy and they shun him. But he believes in his dream and digs up his cornfield to build the baseball diamond. I won't spoil the end of the movie for you, but more than one dream gets fulfilled because Ray 'builds it' or manifests the field of dreams.

There's another 'field of dreams' emerging in the world today, and it's not just from a lone individual like Ray Kinsella. It is a dream that is arising in business leaders, entrepreneurs, educators, religious and spiritual leaders, writers, speakers and social activists. It is a dream of a world that works for all, one where there is peace, justice, ecological balance and a valuing of diversity. Friedensreich Hundertwasser said, 'The dream of one person is just a dream. Dreaming together is the start of a new reality.'

In this dream that we are dreaming together, many of us believe that business is playing a key role in the realisation of this new reality. John Hormann stated this explicitly in his book with Willis Harman, *Creative Work*: 'Business, the motor of our society, has the opportunity to be a new creative force on the planet, a force which could contribute to the well-being of many.' Businesses employ the best and brightest people and invest well in developing their skills. Businesses span global boundaries and are more powerful than most governments. They have developed tremendous problem-solving skills. As our sense of Oneness and interconnectedness on this planet grows, it will become more and more natural for businesses to put these resources to bear on the global challenges we face as a human race such as climate change, antibiotic resistant diseases, food shortages, religious wars, and economic and social inequalities.

It will take enlightened leaders in enlightened businesses to make these kinds of contributions, and this book gives many examples of how that is happening already. We are evolving as a human race, and a shift in global consciousness is taking place in all aspects of our lives, including business. You might ask how this could possibly be, when all we see in the news is story after story of fraud, deception, corruption and greed. The fact is that these are the kinds of things that make news, and that stories about enlightened leaders and organisations don't sell newspapers or television advertising. Nonetheless, it is a quiet revolution that is taking place, and you wouldn't know about it unless you start looking for these positive examples.

I call these leaders 'Edgewalkers' because they walk between the spiritual world and the practical world of everyday business. They have adopted many of the practices and mindsets that Joolz Lewis describes in this book, and have become very successful as a result. Other people have called them boundary spanners, corporate shamans, difference makers and tempered radicals. We are all pointing to the same thing and it is this: spirituality makes a positive difference in leaders and in business. We are not talking about religion, although religion is a beautiful source of spirituality, we are talking about the deep values that Joolz Lewis describes in this book, and we are talking about universal spiritual practices that make one a better person.

If you wanted to find examples of enlightened leaders and enlightened businesses, where would you start looking? There are a number of organisations which are holding events that bring together these enlightened leaders to tell the stories of their companies. One good example is the Conscious Capitalism Institute, founded by John Mackey, Chief Executive Officer of Whole Foods Market. Other organisations include Ashoka, the Social Venture Network, the European Baha'i Business Forum, the Tyson Center for Faith and Spirituality at Work, the Princeton Faith and Work Initiative, MODEM and the International Association of Management, Spirituality and Religion.

It's one thing to hear these leaders tell their stories, and it's a whole different thing to figure out what you might do in your own organisation. It does help to have these examples to show that it really is possible to live spiritual values in the workplace and to demonstrate that spiritual practices really do make you a better leader. That's the first step – believing that it is possible.

But then there is the hard work of figuring out how to live your spirituality in your day-to-day leadership. How do you actually live spiritual values such as service, compassion, authenticity and joy in your work? How can these be incorporated into your strategic planning? Your marketing? Your relationships with your employees? With the creative development of new products and services?

Joolz Lewis first had to figure out both the questions and the answers to these questions for herself when she was an employee in the corporate world and was at the same time following her spiritual path. This book is based on her personal experience, on her studies of best practices in enlightened organisations and on her work with her clients. You will be inspired by her wisdom, and motivated by the down to earth practicality of the actions you can take to be an enlightened leader. My prayer is that you take this book to heart and that you put at least some of these ideas into practice in your own workplace. The effects of your enlightened actions will ripple forth and touch more people than you can ever imagine.

Judi Neal, PhD
6 January 2014, Fayetteville, Arkansas, USA

PREFACE

In the words of the great Martin Luther King, 'I have a dream'.

My dream is one of a business world where people truly care about their work because it is meaningful. A business world in which potential becomes real, where people are supported to be the very best they can be. It is a world that leaves a legacy, contributing in small and large ways to the world in which we live – both in our own communities and beyond.

I dream of a business world which recognises that financial performance is not the only indicator of success – the pursuit of happiness and fulfilment is also worthwhile.

I've worked with hundreds of professionals who share this dream. They want more from their work. They want to inspire others, to change people's lives, to be more fulfilled and ultimately to know that when they shut down for the day they've done more than just line the owner's or shareholders' pockets. This is *sustainable* success.

Never has the business world been so vilified. The financial scandals of the last few years have twisted the public's mind into believing that business and enterprise are fundamentally greed-driven; a view that is sadly only too easy to understand. The upside is that we have a huge opportunity to change – it *is* possible for business to be a force for good, and it *is* possible for business leaders to make a difference.

I've worked as a business consultant for most of my career, nearly 20 years. In my mid-twenties I relocated to work on a contract in what was then jokingly referred to as 'Cisco Valley' in San Jose, California. That contract led to others, and for nearly five years I worked round the clock, spending huge chunks of time on the road, and living the all-consuming American dream. Somewhere in the mix, my personal life fell apart, my nervous system was a wreck and I lost all sense of perspective of who I was, or what the point of it all was. For a while, my saving grace was yoga, and a community centre in Northern California to which I retreated at weekends. But after months of living a schizophrenic life – Monday to Friday 'corporate chick', Saturday to Sunday 'hippy chick' – I woke up one Monday morning with a very clear voice telling me it was time to 'let it go' and move on. I had nothing to move on to, and had a lot to lose – a beautiful apartment two blocks from the Pacific Ocean in Santa Cruz, and a visa that was tied to my work. For a few days I tried to ignore it, but it was insistent, and in my heart I knew that this voice was coming from a deep place of inner wisdom, and that to ignore it would lead to greater problems and pain. Just a week later I handed in my resignation, let go of the flat, sold most of my belongings and packed up what was left into my Subaru, out of which I travelled and camped out in the redwoods for close to a year. It was a wonderful year of freedom, self-discovery, beautiful landscapes and friendship. I completed a yoga teacher-training course, spent three weeks in the Andes, and was blown away by creative insanity at the Burning Man festival in Nevada. It was also during this time that I met my teacher, Amma, from India, who to this day is my spiritual guide.

Back in the UK, the visa having expired, I was convinced that working in business meant having to 'sell my soul'. I fought against it by teaching yoga, but after a while I missed the challenge of consulting, the satisfaction of working with people, delivering value and making a difference in my own small way. Finding 'work–life balance' became a quest for integration – a deep intent to weave together my love for business, and my belief that each of us has a higher purpose, and that this can be expressed through the workplace as 'worthwhile work'. Spirituality is not separate from life, and life is not separate from work. So I decided to go my own way and become an independent consultant.

Why *Enlightened Business*? For a start, enlightened has two meanings that complement each other – one is grounded in the material, physical world we live in, while the other has a spiritual context:

1 | Having or showing a rational, modern and well-informed outlook.

2 | Spiritually aware; the action or state of attaining or having attained spiritual knowledge or insight.

In the context of business, we need leaders with a radical, modern and well-informed outlook to respond to the challenges the world faces today. I believe that age-old, universal spiritual principles can support this process. By universal, I mean faith-neutral, not tied to a particular religion or culture. Rather than being 'other-worldly', these principles can be used in a very real and human way to bring people together, to create more values-driven business, to share more wealth and to treat the planet and its limited resources with respect.

Sadly for many people, the word 'spiritual' can be so closely tied to religion that it creates an immediate barrier. To reference Cindy Wigglesworth's excellent book *SQ21: The Twenty-One Skills of Spiritual Intelligence*, her definition of spirituality is 'the innate human need to be connected to something much larger than ourselves, something we consider to be divine or of exceptional nobility'. Cindy's research shows that the noble qualities we often admire in spiritual leaders are qualities that we have within ourselves, and that these can be developed. In the same way, while the term 'enlightened' is often used to denote the 'end point' of a spiritual quest or journey, it is also the starting point – our innate nature.

In writing this book I am 'standing on the shoulders of giants'. Walking a path that many elders have walked before me. For many years it was the

'Spirit in Work' movement, from which one evolution has been 'conscious capitalism', supported by many notable business leaders, including John Mackey of Whole Foods Market. My sincere hope is that enlightened business contributes to the existing dialogue and work already underway. Whether you prefer the term enlightened, conscious or sustainable business, they all represent different aspects of the same fundamental message: that more and more people are recognising the need for change; and more and more business leaders want to make a difference, leave a legacy and bring fundamental human values back into the business world. If you've picked up this book, that most probably includes you.

This book is not intended to be a theological discourse or academic treatise – I'm simply not qualified to write one. Each chapter is written to offer a new perspective, and provoke self-reflection. I offer it as a bridge between timeless spiritual principles, and the leadership challenges you are facing today. Broadly speaking the part on 'purpose' deals with the strategic aspect of leadership, the part on 'presence' with the day-to-day relationship aspect of leadership (to yourself and others), and the part on 'potential' on creating a culture that is the glue to hold it all together.

You may notice that there is no chapter on 'love'. I simply couldn't separate love out from all the other parts – to me it is the essence of spirituality itself, and all of the qualities outlined help us to tap into that love. By connecting with any and all of the principles outlined, love – which is available to us in the same way that a bulb is always connected to electricity regardless of whether it is switched on – flows freely. When we are in flow with love, we are happier, healthier and more productive.

Whether you have a formal spiritual practice, faith and religious belief or not, the principles in this book are universal. The language may be new to you, but if you read with an open mind and heart you'll see that if you want to be a leader who makes the business world a force for good, then you need to work from the 'inside out'. You *can* have profit *and* make a contribution. It's not so much about *what* you do on a day-to-day basis, it's about *why* it matters, and *how* you do it.

Many years ago I thought my dream was mine alone, and I carried it in my heart until the whisper found the courage to be a voice. Now I know with absolute certainty that this is not 'my' dream – it is a movement, one in which you, I and perhaps millions of others are a part of. Together, one individual at a time, we *can* change the business world – if we are willing to commit to our purpose, be fully present in the process and embrace the potential that is available to us – right now.

ACKNOWLEDGEMENTS

So many people over the years have helped contribute to this book, in many places and in many ways. I feel extraordinarily blessed to be surrounded by so much love and support, and by such a wide and diverse number of communities.

Thanks to all the colleagues and clients I have worked with over the years, who always encouraged me to embrace my quirkiness, and to never compromise on my beliefs and values. Back in the days of being employed, Joe Stuckey and his wife Debbie supported me through my existential quest while I commuted between San Jose and Houston; and David Woodhead demonstrated never-ending patience with my multiple requests for sabbaticals and time out – thank you. To Mark Lavender, Andrea Hughes and Arvi Chana for being wonderful (and fun) teammates.

More recently, Doug Crawford has given me space to bring these principles to life, with year-on-year results showing that they really do work. Likewise Janet Jenkins and Emma Vernon, loyal clients who have valued an alternative approach. I thank you for your trust and your affection.

To all the spiritual and business mentors I have been blessed to work with over the years – some of whom I have never met in person. Special thanks to Nick Williams for giving me the support and advice I needed when setting out right at the start.

To my book designer and dear friend Debi Ani, I always appreciate our way of working and co-creating. Thanks for such a beautiful book design - as always. To Sue Richardson, my wonderful editor and publisher, for giving me as much time and guidance as I needed to 'walk my talk' and allow the content to emerge in its own time. To Jane Gunn, for your generosity in mentoring me as I took my first fledgling steps as a speaker on this topic.

To all my Edgewalking colleagues and friends around the world – you are my tribe. To Judi Neal for inspiring me to connect in the first place, and for your generous foreword. To Kimberly Gunn for your extraordinary grace and presence, and for creating the perfect incubator in Mallorca for this book to emerge. To Sandra, Jan, Marta y Roel and all the other wonderful Edgewalkers who have journeyed along this path with me at various stages – I love you all.

To my 'Amma family', for always being there on this roller coaster ride. In your own individual ways you have all helped me: to Roya, for teaching me the meaning of true friendship; to Tom and Pat for your never-ending unconditional support; to Christa and Kripalu – quietly ever-present; to Charu for friendship that continually transcends physical boundaries; to Shalini – just for being you; Vandita and Meredith and to all my brothers and sisters in the Amma family who pull together every year to put Amma's teachings into practice. Special thanks to Brahmachari Shubamrita for inspiring the opening story – your satsangs are always a joy to listen to, and your life an example in itself.

To the Spirit in Work network, a fabulous community of heart-based consultants and coaches who all share a vision of enlightened business in their own way. To Georgeanne Lamont for leading the charge so many years ago when Spirit in Work was far from mainstream, and for supporting me along every step of my journey.

To the fabulous people I have met through various networking groups, in particular Carrie Bedingfield – a visionary revolutionary who never ceases to amaze and inspire, and Chantal Cornelius for on-tap support and encouragement.

To friends who may not be directly connected with my work, but who 'see' me and cheer me on from the sidelines – especially Andrew, Marleen, Orsola and Millie.

To my parents, Martyn and Corinne, my sister (and best friend rolled into one) Stephanie and brother-in-law Bimal, for never giving up on me when I was 'in the void', and for demonstrating time and again that true love is unconditional. I love you dearly.

To Marcus, for always, always being there and for believing in me.

And finally, to my guiding light Amma, for giving me countless opportunities to overcome my self-doubt, and for showing me so clearly that the only way to change the world is to change oneself.

ONE

◇◇◇◇◇◇◇◇◇◇◇◇◇◇◇◇◇

LEADING FROM PURPOSE

*When you work you fulfil a part of earth's
furthest dream, assigned to you when that dream
was born. Work is love made visible.*

KAHLIL GIBRAN, THE PROPHET

◆

1

PURPOSE: YOUR PERSONAL & BUSINESS MISSION

Follow your bliss.

JOSEPH CAMPBELL

Andrew drove up to the office entrance on his first day as CEO of a hugely successful company. Slightly apprehensive, but eager to get started he pulled to a halt at the security gate. The security guard, who had no idea who Andrew was, asked him for his name and what his purpose was at the business. Immediately, the security guard's supervisor leapt in to apologise to Andrew and usher him through. Later that evening, as Andrew revisited the events of the day in his mind, he recalled the incident with a smile. The next day he requested that he always be asked that question on entering the office – a prompt for him to remember what his true purpose was, beyond showing up for work everyday.

Popular culture does its utmost to convince, coerce and cajole us into believing that the attainment of wealth and material possessions is the secret to happiness. Yet deep down we all know that this is simply not the case, that there is 'something more'. This 'something more' will be different for each of us, but as the field of positive psychology grows, it is becoming clear that there are some common indicators we all share. Our happiness is marked by the quality of our relationships, our contribution to the community and wider society, our freedom, learning and development, fitness and health, leisure time and, above all, *a sense of purpose.*

Your sense of purpose is what gives your life meaning. You have a unique purpose in this life, one that you were born with, waiting for you to claim it. Many people know this, but it can take years of enquiry to truly grasp it, to be able to articulate it with clarity. That's because we're not brought up to think in these terms, we grow up with the expectations of the outside world projected on to us, our impressionable minds absorbing the subtle and not-so-subtle values that accompany the notion of work and career. So much of our thinking and our choices in life stem from this unconscious imprint, an unquestioned assumption that we are defined by our work, our relationships, our living situation and the 'stuff' in our lives – the outside in, rather than the inside out. But an enlightened business leader knows that purpose is at the core of a satisfied life, and focuses time and effort to ensure that work and business support that purpose.

The highest truth according to most spiritual traditions is that, despite appearances, we are not bound by our limited senses and sense of separation; and that by evolving our consciousness we can 'self-realise' and merge into the Oneness that is the source of all of life. If the word Oneness doesn't work for you, I encourage you to replace it with a word that does. Some people prefer the word love, others simply 'life force'. Einstein himself wrote the following:

> A human being is part of a whole, called by us the Universe, a part limited in time and space. He experiences himself, his thoughts and feelings, as something separated from the rest, a kind of optical delusion of his consciousness.

While spiritual teachings have different approaches to achieving this 'end goal', most offer a pragmatic combination of scriptural knowledge to develop 'right thinking' and wisdom; reflection and contemplation to connect with the silence within; and 'love in action' – service to others, helping others less fortunate than ourselves. As individual souls living in a physical plane of existence, we have a purpose to fulfil – as part of that journey, the return to Self. Our life purpose is the manifestation of these practices, the living evidence of our wisdom, reflection and service in action, our focus in the present and our legacy into the future.

Your dreams are calling you uniquely. There is some contribution you can make, some way you can do or be a particular something that is special and unique to you. Your unique, authentic expression is what is demanded here, not someone else's interpretation of who you ought to be.
Rev Deborah L Johnson

Not long ago, most business owners and leaders would have argued that the purpose of business was to make money. Lots of it. But through the boom and bust years, the digital revolution and the increasing focus on customer experience and interaction, more and more people are realising that profit is not the reason but the *result* of good business – the output rather than the starting point.

In many ways, we are talking about a collective version of Maslow's hierarchy of needs. We all know that, at an individual level, we need our physical needs met before we can evolve emotionally and spiritually. In the same way, an organisation also needs to evolve, and as it develops through the various growth stages so it develops its consciousness. This is represented in Table 1 (page 6) – using a model by Richard Barrett, the world expert in values-centred leadership.

At the start-up level, many leaders would say their primary focus is simply to survive financially – to become viable businesses. At the survival and relationship levels, the organisation has grown in numbers, but not necessarily in processes, systems and structure. It can quickly become unsustainable and dysfunctional if it doesn't transform itself into a mature organisation with a broader mission than selling product and making enough profit. So after recognising that what's got them here won't necessarily get them to where they need to go, leaders will look at how they can expand the value chain within their ecosystem – building community both within and without the organisation to make a difference. Finally, an organisation will look at creating a legacy that goes beyond the immediate community

Table 1 | Levels of Organisational Consciousness
Maslow/Barrett's Seven Levels of Consciousness Model

Maslow	Level	Barrett
	7	Service
Self-actualisation	6	Making a difference
	5	Internal cohesion
Know and understand	4	Transformation
Self-esteem	3	Self-esteem
Belonging	2	Relationship
Safety	1	Survival
Physiological needs		

Source: *The Values-Driven Organisation*, Barrett, 2014

they serve, taking into consideration the broadest human, ecological and planetary issues that need addressing. At this point, the organisation becomes a magnet for anyone who shares the same purpose, regardless of whether they are an employee, customer, supplier or immediate stakeholder – they are of service.

Regardless of the stage of growth, enlightened business starts from the inside out, and purpose is the starting point. It is the fundamental driver behind the business, its reason for being and the core of its identity. Oftentimes this is called the business mission. But there's one key difference between how a mission is usually written and structured, and the way in which an enlightened business writes and structures their mission. In old paradigm business, a mission statement would state (usually in quite laboured terms) what it did, and who for. In new paradigm business, the purpose statement is about what the company believes in – its core belief system – and what this means for its stakeholders – staff, customers, suppliers and the wider community.

Increasingly, job seekers and new starters are looking for evidence that the company they are looking to join has a broader social conscience and track record of social responsibility. Research conducted by the non-profit organisation Net Impact showed 53 per cent of workers said that a 'job where I can make an impact' was important to their happiness, and 72 per cent of students about to enter the workforce agreed. With the blurred lines between work life and home life, people want to know that their own values and purpose will be supported by the business environment in which they work. They want community, generosity, learning and growth to be available to them through their work – even in a for-profit environment.

The most deeply motivated people – not to mention those who are most productive and satisfied – hitch their desires to a cause larger than themselves.
Daniel Pink

As a business leader, take this opportunity to revisit your business mission statement. Is it a bland, 'me too' paragraph that would do nothing to inspire the talent or customers you need to attract? Now is the time to refine it. Get input – ask your customers, your board and people from across the company. Find out what's important to them. Conduct an exercise in 'appreciative enquiry' – look at everything that's made you successful up until now. What stands out? What are the themes that crop up again and again that form part of the business DNA? In the same way that individually we all have gifts and talents that make us unique, a business also has a set of attributes that makes it uniquely placed to serve its market in a special way.

The most well-known example of this is Zappos. An online shoe and fashion retailer, Zappos is famous within the field of organisational development for creating a distinctive, quirky culture. However, its mission is 'to inspire the world by showing that it's possible to simultaneously deliver happiness to customers, employees, community, vendors and shareholders in a long-term, sustainable way'. Note, its purpose is not to ship product. For customers, this means exceptional service – 24/7 support, a 365 day return policy (that's right – you can return any goods up to a year after purchase), and free shipping both ways. Everything they do is informed by their purpose – not to make millions (although they did by being bought out by Amazon), but by focusing on happiness. Its founder, Tony Hsieh, has a dream: to create a company where people will perform at their best, and above all, be happy.

When a business has a clear purpose, it unites all the staff who work for it, sends a clear message to customers and helps guide decision making. In the same way that your individual purpose guides your life decisions and actions, so a strong business purpose will guide every aspect of running the business – from how it's structured, to its core activities, and how it communicates internally and externally. ◆

◇◇◇◇◇◇◇◇◇◇◇◇◇◇◇◇◇◇◇◇◇◇◇◇◇◇ **IN A NUTSHELL** ◇◇◇◇◇◇◇◇◇◇◇◇◇◇◇◇◇◇◇◇◇◇◇◇◇◇

1 | At a spiritual level, our purpose is to transcend the limited idea of our self and to discover the 'Oneness' that connects us (including all of nature). Part of the way to do this is by living our lives 'on purpose'.

2 | As we individually evolve our consciousness over time, so does an organisation through various stages of growth (start-up, family, community and tribe).

3 | In enlightened business, purpose is not about making profit – it starts with a mission statement that is clear about what the organisation believes to be important and how that will make a difference (to its industry, its customers, its staff and its stakeholders).

◇◇

2

VISION: DARE TO DREAM

'Would you tell me, please, which way I ought to go from here?' said Alice.
'That depends a good deal on where you want to get to,' said the Cat.
'I don't much care where…' said Alice.
'Then it doesn't matter which way you go,' said the Cat.
'… As long as I get somewhere,' Alice added as an explanation.
'Oh, you're sure to do that,' said the Cat, 'if only you walk long enough.'

LEWIS CARROLL

As a child I was often accused of being a daydreamer; of gazing out of the window, lost in thought; of being 'in my own little world'. How many of us are 'daydream believers'? I can't imagine many managers being thrilled to see staff cloud-gazing while sitting at their desks. And yet taking time to properly and deeply reflect on our dreams and our vision for a better tomorrow *is* necessary. If we don't consciously create the world we step into each morning, then we find ourselves on a metaphorical treadmill, and years pass us by as if we were a silent partner, rather than an active participant. You are a co-creator of your own life, in partnership with an unseen life force that responds to your thoughts and emotions – turning them into the life circumstances that you face each day.

If you could imagine a better tomorrow, what would it look like? Who would benefit? At both a personal and a business level, a vision statement is one that paints a picture of an ideal world. It doesn't matter if you can't see how it's achievable right now. It doesn't have to be tangible or time-bound. Your vision is your opportunity to dream *big*, to play with 'what if', to throw logic and reason to the wind and to say, 'You know what? This is what excites and inspires me. This is what I can get up with a smile for, and this is what I want my life to be about.'

Be audacious. Be bold. Be better.

Notice I'm not saying 'be more'. The era of more money, more things, more stuff is over. Less is more. Time to say 'enough'. If we need more of anything right now, it's more time, more connection through meaningful relationships and conversations, and more insight into what's real.

In a global economy where the effect of crises reverberate around the world, and where each of our actions has an impact far beyond the confines of the community in which we work, we have a responsibility to each and every person on the planet. When the sages talk of 'Oneness', it can so easily be dismissed as an abstract concept – simply because we are not evolved enough to truly experience it in our own personal realities. It's too vast for our limited minds to grasp. But what if we were to start small? What if you were to start with the concept of partnership as part of your dream and vision for a better tomorrow? What would that look like? You don't have to think at the level of the entire world and planet – you can start right where you are.

Start with a clear picture of your ecosystem. Typically, business leaders think of an ecosystem as customers, staff and suppliers. What about the families of these people? What about the community in which you work? Your competitors? Anybody and everybody who touches your business in any shape or form is in your ecosystem. Holding on to your purpose and core beliefs, what is it that you offer that will make a difference to all your stakeholders? How will their lives be different as a result of what you are creating and delivering through your business (or team or function)?

One of my favourite examples of how vision works comes from outside the business world. Every time I visit Barcelona, I am captivated by the Sagrada Familia – the iconic cathedral with its tall and intricate spires reaching for the heavens. But it's not the building that stole my heart; it's the story behind it. A pauper when he died, the architect Antoni Gaudi was run down by a tram, the plans for his masterpiece were on paper and building was not even a quarter complete. Yet nearly 100 years later, building work still continues, and his vision has not just been built, but built upon. It has inspired countless iterations of design, and the result is a masterpiece that will be a living legacy – not just to Gaudi, but to the Catalan spirit and its people. A great vision is one that inspires and engages, that unifies and embodies the spirit of its endeavour.

If you want to build a ship, don't herd people together to collect wood, and don't assign them tasks and work; but rather teach them to long for the endless immensity of the sea.
Attributed to Antoine de Saint-Exupery

Back in the business world, one client is the largest UK provider of home-moving conveyancing – My Home Move. Going through the process of redefining their mission, vision and values, they rejected the standard terminology that many companies use – 'To be the leading...', 'To be recognised as...' etc. Rather than making it all about them, they started from the position of the service they were offering – both to their staff and to their customers. It needed to honour the history of the company in challenging the status quo and being innovative, and it needed to resonate with a young and dynamic staff. Their vision statement is now 'To be conveyancing superheroes'. It's aspirational, memorable and fun – as well as providing plenty of branding opportunity.

Once you have your vision statement, it's tempting to treat it as a tick-box exercise, putting it on the website or in the visitor reception area and moving on to the next important task. But like your purpose statement, it needs to be a living part of your day-to-day life. It's your compass – your North Star that pulls you forward. Make your vision visible – not just in words, but graphically.

We live and work in a world that is shaped and defined by the words we use. Yet shapes, symbolism and colour are necessary to bypass the logical, reasoning part of our brains, freeing up space to be able to dream and believe in the vision, beyond the reality of our day-to-day lives.

A teacher of mine from California once said 'Pain pushes, vision pulls', and I've always found that to be true. When you're stuck, or something's not working, then it gives you the impetus to take action. But your vision is what will pull you forward in the direction you need to go, and it's your vision that will shape the future and inspire others who you need to take on the journey.

If your vision is hazy, unclear or out of date I highly recommend taking time out and doing a simple creative process. This works at both individual and organisational levels – either for your own personal vision or that of the organisation. Collect as many old magazines as you can, ideally from across different fields of interests, with a good selection that reflect your life or industry. Get a large piece of thick card, some scissors and glue. Put on some music and either on your own or as a group, cut out those images and words that leap off the page – the ones that grab you. Just keep cutting and putting the cut-outs to one side. When you've finished going through all the magazines, review the images and words and start laying them out on the piece of card so that they create a storyboard. If you're in a group, discuss why you selected the ones you did and look for links and similarities. When you've selected the ones that most strongly reflect what's most important to you, and the direction you want to take, glue them down on the board. If you're on your own you can take a couple of days, laying out the cut-outs and coming back to them until you're happy with the final picture. Once all the pieces are glued down, frame and hang it – it is now officially a vision board. One client I worked with hung the various versions created by teams on his wall; it was a great conversation starter and lead-in to talk about the company vision. And going back to being a kid with scissors and glue can't be a bad thing! ◆

1 | If you're serious about making a difference through your work or business, give yourself permission to 'think big'. Create space to daydream and imagine what a better world could look like, and how you can contribute to that.

2 | Part of 'dreaming big' is having a wide view of your ecosystem – the extended community in which you work. What could you or your business do differently to how things are currently done in your industry to build a loyal community of supporters who share your beliefs?

3 | Create a personal vision board, or engage with key stakeholders to create a collective one. Make your vision visual. Draw, paint or create a collage. Tap into your creativity to allow the subconscious space to express itself.

◇◇◇

3

FAITH: BELIEFS AND VALUES AS GUIDING PRINCIPLES

It's said,
The sounds that charm our ears
Derive their melody from rolling spheres;
But Faith surpasses the boundaries of doubt,
And sees what sweetens everything.

RUMI

When we hear the word 'faith', it is usually assumed to be in a religious or spiritual context. Faith suggests an irrational belief that requires no proof or evidence, and therefore bypasses the logical mind. In today's secular world, there is certainly little time or tolerance for an exploration of faith in a business context. Fundamentally though, faith is simply an expression of what we believe in – ideally through direct personal experience, but mostly adopted as part of our cultural framework. Beyond the religious or spiritual, we all have faith – a 'worldview' that is based on our life experience; a combination of what we read and see in the physical world, together with what we think and feel about the mystical unseen world – through our senses. Faith gives us strength – when we can't see the way forward it's what keeps us going. It doesn't necessarily have to be placed in a higher power, or invisible being. Put simply, it can be loosely defined as that in which we have complete trust, confidence and belief (whether through direct experience or not).

Our faith has a huge influence on our worldview – it lends itself to a belief system that is lived out on a day-to-day basis through our actions, our choices and our decisions. The bridge between our personal faith and beliefs and the way we interact with others and live our day-to-day lives is our values. As Richard Barrett, the expert in values-based leadership, puts so succinctly, 'Beliefs are contextual and cultural, whereas values are universal. Values transcend contexts, because they arise from the experience of being human.' Another common saying is that 'beliefs divide, values unite'. When looking at how we can embrace different faiths and beliefs in the workplace, we can start with the fundamental truth of our shared humanity, and the common values that transcend cultural limitations and barriers. This is why values-based organisations have shown to be consistently more successful over the years. In the book *Firms of Endearment: How World Class Companies Profit from Passion and Purpose,* the authors Sisodia, Sheth and Wolfe compare the financial performance of Jim Collins' *Good to Great* companies with companies who adopted a conscious capitalism ethos including being values-driven. These outperformed the market and regained their value faster after the 2008 crash, compared to the 'great' companies that over time have proved to be less immune to external market conditions.

Collectively, the values of an organisation reflect 'important and lasting beliefs or ideals shared by the members of a culture about what is good or bad, desirable or undesirable'. In the same way that our own values shape our behaviour, so the organisation's values form the guiding principles regarding 'how things are done around here', and shape its DNA. As an individual's beliefs can be unconsciously inherited from birth, so too can an organisation's – legacy beliefs derived from a previous era, rather than conscious choices that will carry and support its stakeholders on the journey towards its vision. Shared values create connection and community – they bring people together. As a leader, your job is to create an environment that allows people of all faiths to feel welcome, and to work from a set of values that includes everyone within the organisation. Your role is also to ensure that the collective ideals (values) are evident and visible as part of the organisation's purpose.

Values are articulated as words, but lived and breathed on a day-to-day basis. They are demonstrated through attitude, behaviour and language.

One company can have a value that on paper is the same as at another company, but the essence or the meaning is different – depending on the context of its purpose. They are the 'way things are done around here', the fundamental 'how' each action, task and conversation is conducted. They create belonging, and they are the signposts for new people joining, as well as the wider stakeholder group.

So why do so many organisations find it difficult to effectively embed values beyond having the requisite posters on walls? In my experience, it's because it *is* difficult. Consider how hard it is sometimes to make values-based choices just for yourself. Sometimes there's a natural tension between what's easiest and most straightforward, and what you know is right. For example, you may value 'consideration for the planet'. How far does that value stretch? Do you take long-distance flights, or forego the trip? Do you go through the supermarket at the end of a long busy day and deliberately consider the amount of waste packaging? Or do you take shorter showers and fewer baths? Likewise, you may value both 'connection with others' and 'stillness/solitude'. How do you reconcile and balance the two?

Now imagine this on a much, much larger scale. Whether 100, 1,000 or 100,000 employees, the challenge is the same but to the nth degree – how to get everyone on the same page in terms of what the values mean in a very real sense, that is, not just as words on a poster, but in terms of how they govern everyday behaviour and decisions.

When a group of people espouse an agreed set of values and understand which behaviours support those values, then you no longer need to rely on bureaucratic procedures setting out what people should or should not do in specific situations. All the rules reduce to one – live the values.

Richard Barrett, Founder and Chairman of the Barrett Values Centre

Difficult doesn't mean impossible. Nor does it mean it shouldn't be done – for all the reasons above, it's a critical part of leadership, and a strategy in itself. Here are my top ten guidelines to get you off to the best start:

1. Ensure that everyone in the business has input into the definition (or revisiting) of the values – if not the exact wording, the essence of what's important. You can do this via focus groups, 'world café' sessions or at the very least via online survey and questionnaire – although it needs to be carefully worded and backed up by verbal explanation.

2. Define what they mean for the organisation, and at an individual level – values and behaviour are by nature subjective and open to interpretation. So the easier you make it for people to recognise what the behaviour looks like, the less conflict there will be.

3. Weave them through the end-to-end employee lifecycle – from recruitment and induction to coaching conversations and motivational reviews.

4. Assess at what points in your customer journey the values are more challenging to adhere to. For example, you may have seasonal conditions that impact on workload, or there may be a regulatory requirement that conflicts with one of the values. Recognise and raise it openly – open dialogue will help to clarify expectations for those affected.

5. Equip your managers with the skills they need to give values-based behavioural feedback.

6. Live them! (And own where this wasn't possible – individually and at a team and business level.)

7. Define how you'll measure values-based performance, and communicate results the same way you would any other business metric.

8. Yes, posters and visible reminders are important – on their own they are not enough, but they reinforce the importance in the workspace.

9. Reward and recognise – create a reward programme that allows values 'stars' to feel special and publicly recognised. They will become your 'champions'.
10. Take tough action – in extreme cases, there may be people who carry out their tasks and meet targets, but who are disruptive to the culture of the organisation. This is normally because they don't subscribe to the values-set, and as such it needs to be addressed as part of the performance management process.

One of my clients is a forward-thinking property agency called Miller-Metcalfe, a company with huge ambitions for growth, while doing a huge amount of work in the community and committed to leaving a legacy. They have a values-based programme called MPeople that runs through every aspect of the business. While I don't typically recommend more than five values (sometimes it is difficult for staff to differentiate between them or remember them all), they have done a great job in clearly articulating and weaving them through different parts of the business:

G: Giving back
O: Openness
T: Team spirit

P: Professionalism
R: Respect
I: Integrity
D: Different approaches
E: Enthusiasm

MChampions take on board feedback and pass it on to the senior leadership team, and all staff attend a monthly MPeople meeting to give feedback and share ideas. There are also annual awards for those members of staff who have most demonstrated the values.

We can all think of organisations who live and breathe their values, and the difference it makes to employees and customers alike. Faith may not typically be associated with the business world (beyond chaplaincy and a multifaith prayer room) but it shapes an organisation's values and behaviour – the external proof and evidence of what an organisation believes in. Values are fundamental in creating 'conscious business' – business that isn't just about profit, but which honours the individual need for aspiration, human connection and a sense of belonging. ◆

◇◇◇◇◇◇◇◇◇◇◇◇◇◇◇◇◇◇◇◇◇◇◇◇◇◇◇◇◇ **IN A NUTSHELL** ◇◇◇◇◇◇◇◇◇◇◇◇◇◇◇◇◇◇◇◇◇◇◇◇◇◇◇◇◇◇◇◇◇

1 | While faith is typically associated with religion or spirituality, at its simplest it can be interpreted to mean 'what you or an organisation believes to be important'.

2 | Values are universal principles (rather than localised beliefs) that reflect what we believe to be important, and translate into how we think and act on a day-to-day basis.

3 | Taking time to embed values-based behaviour at an organisational level is essential to be credible as a business that does things differently, that is, not growth at any cost, or success at any price, but in the right way.

◇◇

4

ALIGNMENT: SOW THE SEEDS AND PLAN

If you can tune into your purpose and really align with it, setting goals so that your vision is an expression of that purpose, then life flows much more easily.

JACK CANFIELD

So, you know where you're going – your vision. You know what your core purpose is – your mission. You have faith in the endeavour and the people you work with, and you know what your personal and collective values are. Great! But how do you bridge the present and the future? Although the vision and mission can sometimes be worded in future terms, for example 'To be....', 'We will...', it is the starting point, the here and now out of which all action emerges.

Living your way into the future means ensuring there is alignment between your present reality and your future vision. Every thought you think, word you say and action you take are like seeds being planted in fertile ground, waiting for the right conditions to develop and bear fruit. You can't force the process any more than you can force a rose to bloom before it's ready to unfold. Neither do we have a crystal ball that allows us to see all the external factors and conditions that will impact on our business plans. As the saying goes, 'We make plans; God laughs.' Yet in our role as 'co-creators' we are responsible for taking action, for planning our way into the future in a way that creates alignment between what we declare the business purpose and vision to be, and the steps we're taking towards it. In reality, in every moment we are pulling the future forward, and living it in the now.

A friend of mine, Roel Simons, is a wonderful social documentary film-maker who has launched a project called 'Journal of the Future'. He invites people to live out the future as if it were the present – literally asking them to use the language, take action and start acting as if the future were already here. What would that look like for you? What language would you be using? What would you be doing differently?

In my experience there are three types of business. The first espouses the 'just do it' philosophy. It sounds like a good idea, there's an opportunity there, so let's just go for it. Rarely do they stop to consider how it fits with the core purpose of the organisation, how it will impact on existing work commitments or what the risks are. The leadership team probably comprises 'starter' creative types, rather than 'completer' disciplined types. This type of business is more likely to be owner-led, started small and is still operating with a start-up mentality even though they've grown in size.

On the other end of the scale, there are businesses who spend so much time planning, creating business cases and conducting risk analysis that they are late to market and miss the boat. These tend to be the larger corporates who are weighed down by multiple priorities, convoluted communication channels between different departments, and (sadly) personal and political agendas.

The 'enlightened business', however, is a combination of the two. As a leader of this type of business or function, you recognise the need to reflect and take stock before taking action. You take time to ask fundamental questions such as 'What are the options here?', 'How will this impact on current operations, workload and staff fulfilment?', 'What would happen if we did nothing?' You consult with key stakeholders within the organisation, and external contacts who have relevant expertise. It doesn't take months to do this, just a few days or at most a few weeks to ensure that you're making the best decision. This is the phase that I call 'sowing the seeds'. It's the phase of ensuring the soil is fertile before taking action. Every thought and conversation is creating the future outcome, even before the first task is completed.

Judge each day not by the harvest you reap but by the seeds you plant.
Robert Louis Stevenson

Once this is done you can start the actual planning – what needs to happen, by who and when. This is where the critical element of alignment comes in to play.

There isn't one area of our life or work where we operate as an independent entity. Every single word and action has an impact on the world around us and the people in it. That's quite a responsibility. Once again, if this is true at an individual level, imagine how much more powerful it is at a collective level. In order to ensure that everyone in the organisation is working towards the same end goal, you need alignment, which means:

- Every employee and team member knows how their own role contributes to the 'greater good' and core purpose of the organisation.
- Every employee and team member knows, at least at a high level, what the 'critical path' to achieving the end vision looks like – that is, the initiatives, programmes and projects that are underway. If it's a large corporate business, then this should be true of the business unit within which they work.
- Project managers focus as much on the impact of change on various aspects of the business (systems, process, behaviour) as they do on completing the project on time, to budget etc.
- The senior leadership team review the high level plans on a regular basis to ensure that no conflict exists between deadlines and priorities.
- As plans are developed and projects implemented, the right people are consulted at the right time, and the right people are informed when they need to be. This is done with respect for day-to-day workload considerations, and with enough advance notice that there is no adverse impact on 'business as usual' activity.

Planning is a necessary part of business management, and no leader would be expected to run a business or function without an element of planning. It helps structure thinking, communicates expectations and requirements of others, and it facilitates reporting of progress towards the end goal. But planning is a tool, a means to an end rather than the end in itself. An enlightened leader isn't a slave to the plan; and in considering how to align with the broader business objectives and the organisation as a holistic entity, it is a living document that needs to remain fluid and responsive to changing conditions and emerging opportunities.

Planning is bringing the future into the present so you can do something about it now.
Alan Lakein

As you awake each day and transition from your family and home life to the desk, take a moment to consider how you are 'living the future'. Moment to moment we are living our way into the future, and in each moment we have the opportunity to create a different outcome. Sow the seeds on a daily basis, plan based on what you know today and align yourself with your team, organisation and environment. ◆

◇◇◇◇◇◇◇◇◇◇◇◇◇◇◇◇◇◇◇◇◇◇◇◇◇◇ IN A NUTSHELL ◇◇◇◇◇◇◇◇◇◇◇◇◇◇◇◇◇◇◇◇◇◇◇◇◇◇

1 | In each moment we are living our way into the future. Planning is a mechanism to ensure alignment between our day-to-day activity and our future vision.

2 | Every thought and action we take in the present is like a seed being planted for the future.

3 | Planning is a fundamental aspect of business management. However, as well as delivering the stated objective, plans need to ensure alignment at all levels, and be flexible enough to allow for change along the way. Planning is the means to the end, not the end itself.

◇◇◇

5

TRUTH: SELL WITH INTEGRITY

Three things cannot be long hidden; the sun, the moon and the truth.
BUDDHA

Truth. A five-letter word that has been misunderstood and abused for millennia. Over the centuries, it has been the quest of spiritual seekers across all cultures, and yet the cause of countless atrocities in the name of religion. It is mostly subjective – my truth may not be the same as yours. It is heavily influenced by our values and belief systems – hence it is often seen in a subjective light, an interpretation rather than an objective universal law.

The goal of each religion is the same. It is the absolute, transcendent state, the one Reality, the eternal Truth… This is the goal not only of all religion, but of all human existence.
Bede Griffiths

The truth that I believe in, the spiritual belief underpinning most of the world's religions, is that we are all 'One'. That while externally we differ wildly in terms of physical characteristics, language, belief, behaviour and norms, there is an underlying consciousness that unifies us all – an essence that is the life force, which doesn't differentiate between race, colour or creed. But as long as we are bound to this physical body, what we see with our physical eyes undermines that truth – because we see no hard evidence of it on a day-to-day basis. Rather, we don't look for it, so we don't see it. It doesn't matter what religion you practice, or what the name of your god is, we all came from Source, and will return to Source. But we get hung up on the differences, and the small individual 'truths' that we all carry around with us – the limiting beliefs and behaviours that separate us from each other.

Unfortunately, this is all too clear in the world of business. Mini-fiefdoms operate across an organisation, power games are played out and aggressive tactics are used to 'win' (steal) customers from competitors. In a competitive world, where the quest for profit and bonus payouts is the driving force, it's difficult to uphold the universal truth of Oneness. The old paradigm of business would certainly have deemed it impossible, *and* as unnecessary. At the dawning of this new age of business, people are questioning whether it *is* possible – as difficult as it may seem – and some are questioning whether in fact it is a *necessity* for success, because the nature of success is being redefined. Whereas before it had been limited to the above criteria – financial returns for a few, and no more – it now has a much wider meaning. Employees demand more fulfilment, more flexibility with their work-life (more integration and adaptable working practices), and the sense that they're working for a company that they can be proud to work for. I met an expat in Singapore recently who, in response to my question regarding who he worked for, replied 'an IT company'. It turned out he works for Barclays, but in IT – he was just too embarrassed to say so.

So what does 'truth' look like in business? How can it become a universal principle that drives a company's ethos, and how can it be measured? Translating the spiritual principle and ideal of Oneness into human terms, we can look for qualities that at the very least offer a starting point towards treating everyone fairly and equitably. Let's start with a definition. According to Merriam-Webster, truth is 'sincerity in action, character and utterance'. It is closely linked to the definition of integrity: 'a firm adherence to a code of especially moral or artistic values'. Once again we're back to values. If we can nurture the values of unity, connection and fairness then we'll be on a journey to the ultimate truth – seeing the best in others and others as a mirror of ourselves; wanting the best for all, not just a favourite few.

On an individual basis, only we and those we work with closest can know if we are indeed being 'true'. At a business level, it's most often the sales organisation that drives the reputation of the business, and that illustrates most closely the extent to which the organisation is one of truth, integrity and sincerity. Over the last few years, the financial services industry has taken a hammering for mis-selling; stories of elderly people being sold unnecessary insurance products, and the collapse of people's retirement funds while 'fat cat' bosses walk away with millions has rightly incensed us. But it's not just the financial services industry. Multinational super-giants across multiple sectors have set themselves up in such a way as to maximise tax loopholes, giving them a huge advantage over local small businesses.

In his book, *Principled Selling: How to Win more Business without Selling your Soul*, David Tovey writes:

> *Having integrity is easy on good days, when things are going well and there are no difficult choices to make. The real test is on those difficult days when behaving in a way that is consistent with your proclaimed values has a perceived cost. Every one of the corporations and financial institutions that let us down during the banking crisis had fine sounding values and corporate social responsibility policies prominently displayed on their websites and in their marketing materials. The problem was not the proclaimed values and principles; it was that some of them had no integrity.*

Is this really likely to change? Only if consumers like you and me walk away with our feet and our wallets. But more importantly, let's not forget that while the big names may grab the headlines, for every one large name that is shamed, there are hundreds if not thousands of businesses who do sell with integrity. The managing director of one client of mine believes that there should only be one value in his business – integrity – and turns down deals that aren't right for the company. I recently heard of a company that found itself in a difficult sales conflict: they were simultaneously selling to American Tobacco and Cancer Research. While they were debating their own ethical boundaries, Cancer Research got wind of it and made their decision for them – they walked.

It takes 20 years to build a reputation and five minutes to ruin it. If you think about that, you'll do things differently.
Warren Buffett

Even if you're not paid as a salesperson, if you are in a customer-facing role of any description, the way you interact and represent your company will be a reflection of how it sells itself. So how can you sell with integrity and 'walk the talk'?

- Define why integrity matters to you – individually, and as a function or organisation.
- Identify all customer 'touch points' where integrity can and should be demonstrated, and what this would look like.
- Be honest – where's the gap? Look at your communication, proposals and contracts and look at how you could be more honest and 'true' to your prospects and customers. Is integrity covered in your sales training?
- Lay down very clear guidelines regarding when a 'deal at any cost' is not acceptable, what the 'walk away' points are and why. Reasons include brand reputation, ongoing service and fulfilment costs, or account management overheads.
- Monitor and report – celebrate and highlight examples of integrity-led behaviour as much as the sales figures. The message will get through.

Ultimately, you and your organisation will be more successful if you follow your truth – your beliefs and values, and demonstrate integrity and make the hard decisions when necessary – even if it means missing sales targets. Doing the right thing leads to trust, and trust leads to longer-term more rewarding relationships. And that, in the long run, is what will keep you going through the tough times and into the good. ◆

4 | The spiritual truth underpinning most religions is that we are all One. In human terms, this means seeing beyond the differences and honouring all life forms with respect.

5 | In business, being truthful means acting with integrity – where everyone in the organisation (including, and especially, the sales function) follows a moral code of conduct.

6 | As a business leader, review your processes and be honest about where there are opportunities for integrity to slip. People don't set out to be less than truthful, but the structure and culture of an organisation needs to support people in bringing their best and highest selves to work. Your reputation depends on it.

◇◇◇

6

SERVICE: A HIGHER PURPOSE

If Firms of Endearment can be described by any one characteristic, it is that they possess a humanistic soul. From the depths of this soul, the will to render uncommon service to all stakeholders flows. These companies are imbued with the joy of service – to the community, to society, to the environment, to customers, to colleagues.

SISODIA, SHETH AND WOLFE

Service is a broadly used term. A church 'service' refers to the act of communal worship. A funeral 'service' is a ritual to honour the departed. A public 'servant' is one who has chosen a career in service of the wider society. When a car needs a 'service', it's time for it to get some much needed tender loving care. In some countries 'national service' is mandatory (conversely in Thailand a few months in a monastery are required), and in business, service typically refers to the post-sales support function.

In all cases it refers to the offering of help. Whether it's in a voluntary, vocational or professional capacity, service is about being of use, of helping others and of offering one's time and talents to make a difference in some way. In all spiritual traditions, being of service and helping others is a bedrock of the teachings. Each has its philosophy and scripture, and most promote regular contemplation and times of stillness. But unless you're a monk or a renunciate living in a cave, putting the philosophy and teachings into practice in our day-to-day lives is essential to further our spiritual development.

This was, for me, the biggest lesson learned after returning to the UK from an extended period of yoga study and practice. Up until that point I had been entirely focused on my own spiritual growth through hours of yoga postures, meditation, breathing techniques and various fasts. I confess that voluntary service had never been a part of my life – not having been a member of any local church community, nor having had exposure to voluntary projects, it never occurred to me that service was something I could do on a day-to-day basis. I thought it was reserved for missionary-type people, 'human saints' who had a calling for vocational work. I respected it, but it was for other people, not me.

No work is meaningless. It's the amount of heart — of love — that is poured into the work that determines how meaningful it is.
Amma

That all changed once I started to become clearer regarding the true message of the *vedic* scripture and teachings from India. Service is an attitude that translates into action. It's the attitude behind the action that determines whether it is of service or not — it's about intent. If your intent is to serve through your every action, it doesn't matter what you're doing, it's an offering to the world. This took some time to get my head around. While I spent endless days configuring customer relationship management (CRM) databases, defining business requirements and developing training modules, wondering how on earth I could make the world a better place, all along, I slowly realised, it was about my attitude towards the work and the people I worked with that determined the outcome. So the great news was that I didn't need to give it all up (again!) and become a charity worker in a war-torn part of the world. It wasn't my calling; in fact my calling was exactly right where I already was — in the business world.

So how can you and your organisation be of service? In my experience, the more customer-focused a business is, the more likely it is to have a service ethos at its core. A while back I carried out a 'service excellence' initiative for a client whereby I held short sessions with every function in the business, helping them to identify their purpose, who their immediate and ultimate customers were and how they served them. In concrete terms they were able to see how they contributed to the big picture, and internal functions with no direct contact with the customer were able to see how their role still served the end client. This is a fundamental starting point, to help everybody at each level of the organisation appreciate the interconnectedness of their role and function, and have an appreciation of who their customers are.

One of the old business paradigms that needs to shift in order to truly reflect the importance of service is reward and compensation. Too many organisations still structure their bonus payments and commissions with a strong emphasis on sales. Conversely, people in a post-sales 'service' role are often the lowest paid, demeaning the value of service in the organisation and sending the wrong message to staff. When non-sales employees are rewarded equal to their sales colleagues for their part in delivering customer satisfaction and loyalty, then the standard rhetoric of 'customer above all else' will start to ring true.

Jane Sunley, author of *Purple Your People* and founder of Purple Cubed, started her first business in the recruitment industry, typically renowned for paying low salary and high commission. She says:

> We felt it would have been irresponsible to employ people who made important decisions based on how much money they'd make; placing people into jobs just because it swelled the monthly paycheck. Competitors scoffed at this naivety… however this ethical and honest stance won over both clients and candidates and we were extremely successful. We paid fair salaries plus an annual profit share which everyone, sales focused or not, could benefit from on a fair basis. We retained people, they were highly motivated and so they bettered their targets.

But beyond the customer, employees also want to know that they are part of something bigger than themselves, something that helps them feel their work is worthwhile. Obviously this starts with them – if they give of their best, are willing to help others and go the extra mile when necessary, they will be fulfilled. But meaningful corporate social responsibility (CSR) programmes are increasingly playing a bigger role in shaping an organisation's brand and philosophy. SalesForce.com, a cloud computing company, was set up with philanthropy a priority from the start, and gives each employee six days of paid time a year for voluntary work. In his book *Compassionate Capitalism* with Karen Southwick, its founder, CEO and chairman, Marc Benioff cautions against waiting until the company is 'big enough' to start making a difference:

> *The new model says that philanthropy must be woven into every thread of corporate existence so that it becomes a part of the cultural fabric and cannot be pulled out without pulling apart the corporation itself. Organisations that have service as a core value of their culture will see both intrinsic and external returns... It is simply part of being human to be able to give, and companies that provide the opportunity will find that it energises employees and executives.*

Nor does this concept apply only to multimillion international corporations. The most inspiring example of a business with a service ethos at its core is a company I came across in the USA a few years back. Televerde in Phoenix, Arizona, is a business-to-business (B2B) marketing agency that employs convicted female offenders – offering them an opportunity to develop new skills and gain experience so that they are more employable on leaving prison. They also set up TENS – the Televerde Endowment for New Scholars – to empower women who are re-entering society to realise their life goals through higher education. In the UK, companies such as Legal & General are also taking a harder look at how they can partner with charities, rather than just ticking a box with volunteering hours.

If you are in a business that is currently too small to initiate or manage your own volunteering or funding initiative, I highly recommend you check out 'Buy1GIVE1' (www.b1g1.com), a really simple programme that connects small businesses to give to a project of their choice, with donations made every time a customer spends money with them. Just to reinforce what I've been writing about in terms of defining what you believe in, and the importance of giving back, this is what its founder Masami Sato has to say. She calls it 'The Power of Small':

We believed that if giving was made simple, easy and truly impactful, every business would want to give back to make a difference. Giving doesn't have to be a result of success. We wanted to make giving a part of our business journey. Imagine if every time you had a meal, a hungry child received a meal...
Or imagine if every time you had a cup of coffee, someone received access to life-saving water...
Or imagine if every time you bought a book, a tree got planted...
I'm certain that every business is founded for a reason; to bring a sense of joy to people; so that they can work on creating great value while doing what they love to do.

This lies at the heart of what Harvard Business School Professors Porter and Kramer called 'Creating Shared Value' (CSV). The objective is both company and community value generation, and applies a more integrated, holistic approach which means that service and 'doing good' is integrated into the fabric of the business – rather than it being a sideline activity that can be opted in or out. My sense is that, increasingly, companies will need to adopt the CSV approach in order for their vision of service to be meaningful and truly worthwhile. It takes a visionary sense of how the business can contribute to society in a bigger way, what its role is in the local community, and the courage to take real action towards it. ◆

1 | Service isn't just a post-sales function – it's an attitude that everyone in the organisation should share.

2 | The old-paradigm commission structure that rewards sales for bringing in new business, rather than sharing it equally with those who service and retain customer loyalty, needs to be looked at if companies are serious about valuing its staff and customers.

3 | CSV is about putting 'giving back' at the heart of the business – as part of its strategy – rather than as a sideline activity.

◇◇◇

7

DISCIPLINE AND SURRENDER:
FROM COMMAND AND CONTROL TO TRUST

You cannot fulfil God's purposes for your life
while focusing on your own plans.

RICK WARREN

For many people, the word discipline is loaded with negative connotations – childhood memories of punishments being doled out at school and at home, of being forced to do household tasks and homework rather than being free to play and run wild. In the world of work, however, it is a critical quality. It is the foundation of a good work ethic – the discipline to manage one's time, behaviour and language. When you have a strong purpose and vision, and a plan to get there, the traditional business belief is that all it takes is focus and discipline to stick to the plan and reach the goal. But is it really that simple?

In most of the faith traditions, discipline is a quality that is strongly encouraged. This takes many forms – physical discipline such as abstinence from harmful substances, and regular exercise to maintain health; and mental discipline in terms of the ability to control one's thoughts and emotions. Spiritual practices such as yoga and meditation were designed specifically with this objective – to allow the body and mind to work in harmony towards the higher goal.

Arduous is the path, as difficult to tread the sharp edge of a razor, so say the wise.
The Upanishads

The ancient scriptures of India refer to the spiritual path as similar to 'walking the razor's edge'. It is that difficult – because it takes more than discipline. It takes self-awareness, patience, a willingness to learn, to forgive – and to surrender.

Surrender is probably an even less popular a word today than discipline. It is often viewed as a weakness: not holding one's ground or being willing to let go in the face of adversity. But in the spiritual sense, surrender is about both trust and acceptance. Acceptance of our current reality, no matter how different it may look from our future aspirations; and trust that as long as we're showing up to the best of our ability, doing the right thing and listening for guidance, then the right path will unfold as we step forwards. It may not always look the way we had anticipated, or even wished for – but surrender means being willing to let go of any preconceived ideas of what an outcome will look like. It means accepting that we don't operate within a vacuum – as any strengths, weaknesses, opportunities and threats (SWOT) or political, economic, social, technological, legal and environmental (PESTLE) analysis will tell you – and that, ultimately, we are not in control.

By letting it go it all gets done. The world is won by those who let it go. But when you try and try, the world is beyond the winning.
Lao Tzu

In the book *Living Leadership*, the authors Binney, Wilke and Williams argue that one of the fundamental shifts in leadership today is the need to let go of the idea of being a 'transformational hero'. Yes, vision and future strategy are important, but it's all about leading within context: the day-to-day successes, issues and interpersonal dynamics that shape an organisation. Inspiring a great dream and sense of possibility is important – but you don't want to be so divorced from the current reality that your vision is referred to as a 'hallucination'. So the discipline is in balancing the future aspiration and belief in the potential of the business, while surrendering and adjusting to where the business is now.

It is part of a normal human process to dream great dreams, to work hard for them and find that what you create is not quite what you expected. The capacity to articulate your aspirations and the self-belief to want to put them into practice is essential to leadership, but so is the ability to adjust to reality and learn as your story unfolds.
Binney, Wilke and Williams

I once learned this the hard way. A few years back I joined the local Chamber of Commerce Council, encouraged to do so by Georgeanne Lamont, a colleague who I respected and admired greatly. She was president at the time, and the council consisted of a group of wonderfully talented, energetic, inspired and generous individuals who shared a vision for a thriving and successful business community, with the Chamber at its heart. We had a vision statement and strategy, we partnered with local government bodies, and educational institutions to engage with youth, and launched a flagship breakfast networking event with high-profile speakers that, we believed, set the bar for the Chamber moving forwards.

The problem was that while we had one Chamber employee on the Council, we weren't fully integrated with the organisation. We didn't appreciate the culture of the Chamber, or seek to find 'middle ground' between where we wanted to be and what the current reality of the Chamber was. In addition there were political considerations with the launch of the new Local Enterprise Partnerships (LEP) that were taking up a huge amount of resource and attention internally – meaning that we were thwarted in some of our larger endeavours. But with surrender comes an awareness of other opportunities that may be available – and more often than not right under our noses. At least one of my fellow council colleagues is now involved with the local LEP, to the benefit of his business.

We must be willing to let go of the life we have planned, so as to have the life that is waiting for us.
Joseph Campbell

Ultimately, surrender requires trust. Trust is usually used in the context of belief in someone or something – often distinguished from faith by having had a precedent to do so. In other words it's not 'blind' but established through previous behaviour or conditions. When it comes to surrender, it takes both trust in our own intuition – our ability to sense what is required of us from day to day (even if it's not in the plan) – along with trust that 'all will be well', even if we can't see how. It means first acknowledging, and then accepting, the circumstances the business finds itself in and then responding to that – even if it's unfamiliar territory. The high street is littered with relics in the retail space who lacked the discipline to constantly challenge themselves in the assumptions and choices they were making. They also failed to surrender to what the digital age meant to their business – which in turn led to a catastrophic failure to adapt and respond accordingly. Acceptance that the situation may not be what you want is the first step, then having the trust that the organisation has the capacity to still find a way forward is key.

In leading from purpose, we have explored the meaning of purpose and the importance of creating a vision that is shaped and informed by the current reality. We have looked at the importance of ideals and values, of integrity and service, discipline and surrender. The ability to keep one eye on the future with both feet fully grounded in the present is also an essential leadership quality. This takes presence – the bridge between purpose as the internal driver and the potential wanting to unfold.

Always say 'yes' to the present moment. What could be more futile, more insane, than to create inner resistance to what already is? What could be more insane than to oppose life itself, which is now and always now? Surrender to what is.

Say 'yes' to life – and see how life suddenly starts working for you rather than against you.
Eckhart Tolle

1 | Discipline and surrender are essential leadership qualities to ensure that the future vision of the business is balanced with the current day-to-day challenges and realities that it faces.

2 | The best visioning and planning processes in the world can't foresee all circumstances. Surrender means accepting that no business is immune to external influences and that goals may or may not be achieved as anticipated.

3 | Trust means being able to take decisions and actions in the unknown, confident that success will ensue even if it looks different to what was originally intended.

◇◇

TWO

LEADING WITH PRESENCE

The most precious gift we can offer others is our presence.

THICH NHAT HANH

◆

8

COMMITMENT – SHOW UP!

*Ole! to you, just for having the sheer human love
and stubbornness to keep showing up.*

ELIZABETH GILBERT

Being a leader in an 'enlightened business' means making a commitment to your purpose at the core of your being and your life – at a soul level. It's not enough to have a personal mission statement and vision board on your office cubicle or wall. While there are many dimensions to our everyday life and work, we tend only to focus on the physical realm. Yet everything starts as energy, the unseen mystery that precedes form. Values become beliefs, then thoughts, which become words, actions and habits. Essentially, they are how you live your life. When you align your beliefs and thoughts with your purpose, your words, actions and habits can follow in the physical realm. This is known as your deepest intent.

Reverend Deborah Johnson in her book *Your Deepest Intent* says, 'Intent is not merely about goals. Intent is beyond objectives, plans or strategies. Intent is beyond hopes and expectations… intent resides in the depth of your soul.'

The very nature of soul is elusive and intangible. When it lies dormant it can feel lifeless and inert, which is how most people experience it when it's not called upon, when it's not brought into partnership with a life purpose. Conversely, whenever you feel inspired, energised and your work is effortless or 'in flow', then it's evidence of your soul working through you, a key quality of presence. Soul responds to inspiration; it is the seat of creativity and is the portal to the unseen energetic realm where potential resides. So while you may have envisioned your purpose and can sense the *possibility* that lies within it, there is in fact infinite *potential* available to you.

By making a commitment to live from your deepest intent, to partner with your soul and to live in potential, you are aligning the energetic realm of your life with any action you take to show up in the physical world – you are leading with presence.

Commitment is the external expression of intent. It means showing up on a day-to-day basis, taking action in support of your life purpose and mission. Note that this doesn't mean being busy. Millions of people the world over are so busy they're overwhelmed, but this doesn't mean they're showing up. To show up means you take steps towards realising the potential and possibility of your life purpose.

It often means breaking through old patterns of thinking or behaviour that get in the way of you achieving your goals and objectives. For some strange reason, we seem to be programmed to resist our greatest potential. Resistance is a signpost, a sign that there's an area of growth for us to stretch in to, or a place of fear to overcome.

One acronym for fear is 'false evidence appearing real'. Our minds create stories for why something isn't possible, why it's not safe, and tells us that we might make fools of ourselves or get it wrong. When you're showing up, everyday is a supreme act of courage – to be your best self, to stand up for what you believe in, to take responsibility for your life, and to have the conviction that you really are here for a reason, and that you *can* make a difference.

Courage starts with showing up and letting ourselves be seen.
Brené Brown

It's easy to think of inspirational figures such as Martin Luther King and Gandhi who were so dedicated to their cause and purpose that nothing deterred them from it, not even social exclusion and violence. However, such acts of selfless dedication are happening on an anonymous, daily basis all over the world – bomb disposal experts, environmentalists and even leaders within organisations who are so committed to the unfoldment of the declared purpose and mission of the organisation that they put themselves in the line of metaphorical fire.

Before you take action and show up, there may be work to do to uncover and release any energetic obstacles to your purpose. Without being aware of it, we all have programmed thought patterns that can pull us in a different direction to the one we want to move in. How to identify these obstacles and internal barriers to success? Typical signs are procrastination, lethargy, a sense of frustration and unusual emotional outbursts. If a task or project has been on your 'to do' list for longer than a month with no progress, stop to think about what has truly got in the way. Is there a genuine reason, or is it your resistance to doing something that is more worthwhile, and possibly more scary than the familiar and comfortable day-to-day work? Nick Williams in his book *Resisting Your Soul: 101 Tips to Free Your Inspiration* says:

You beat your resistance through a combination of your awareness, your intention and mindset and practical strategies. In essence, you get through resistance by a choice – of making something else more important than fear.

I want to revisit the point made in Part One about planning and alignment. Many leaders believe that showing up means executing a plan, forgetting sometimes that the plan may no longer serve the purpose of the organisation. The key is to remain flexible, to wake up everyday with an awareness of the long-term 'why' and the vision, and then focus the mind on how that translates into what needs to happen this week, and this hour.

But having presence by showing up in service of the purpose and vision on a daily basis isn't enough when you're leading an organisation. It's also about eliciting others' commitment, otherwise progress would be very slow indeed. So not only is leading with presence about showing up yourself, but how you get others to commit to the same vision.

Ultimately, commitment from others is a by-product of engaging with people to involve them in how they envisage the future of the business and their own role within it. In their eyes, your commitment is a given (no matter what battles you may be fighting on the inside), whereas you need to earn and win theirs on an ongoing basis. Showing up in service of your purpose and vision takes daily commitment – to a higher purpose, and to making a difference. Sometimes it's taking those small steps that people may not necessarily notice, and other times it may mean taking giant leaps. But commitment to show up and lead the way translates into presence – when people know what you stand for, what you're working towards and how you interact with others along the way. ◆

◇◇◇◇◇◇◇◇◇◇◇◇◇◇◇◇◇◇◇◇◇◇◇◇ **IN A NUTSHELL** ◇◇◇◇◇◇◇◇◇◇◇◇◇◇◇◇◇◇◇◇◇◇◇◇◇

1 | While you may have a deep intent to realise your purpose and business mission, unless you take concrete steps in the right direction and on a consistent basis, progress and results will be ad hoc and erratic. You need commitment – you need to show up.

2 | You know when you're in flow – when your soul is working through you, when your work feels effortless. You are present. But this may take work to unplug any energetic blocks and resistance.

3 | Gaining others' commitment is just as important. Engaging with them and asking how they envisage the future empowers them to succeed on their own terms, and results in long-term loyalty.

◇◇

9

AUTHENTICITY – GET REAL

*The God who existed before any religion counts on you to make
the oneness of the human family known and celebrated.*

DESMOND TUTU

There's a paradox here, and it's a complex one. The paradox is that
according to metaphysical philosophy and many spiritual traditions, we are
spiritual beings living a human existence and that our 'true' self – beyond
this limited human form – is one with all: infinite Love.

But on the other hand, our experience is mostly defined as human
beings having the occasional spiritual experience. Everywhere around us
we see evidence of less than enlightened behaviour, people hurting each
other, and the unconscious wreaking havoc. In practicing and striving for
the truth of their unlimited being, many spiritual aspirants find themselves
needing to be 'good people' in order to validate their self-identity. Carl
Jung referred to the 'shadow' side of our nature; failure to deal with it can
often mean avoiding conflict, suppressing anger and only seeing the good
in others, rather than being real with our own and others' limitations, and
embracing their individuality. The Chinese represent this balance between
darkness and light in the classic yang–yin symbol.

Regardless of whether or not you consider yourself to be 'spiritual', your
childhood upbringing most probably reinforced the moral importance of
being loving and good, of needing to please others, do the right thing and
do your best at school. We inherit our parents' values and beliefs, and have
little opportunity to consciously evaluate them and choose others that more
accurately reflect who we are. So when we enter the workplace with these
patterns, there's a degree of inauthenticity, of fear of failure and of wanting
to please others rather than be true to ourselves.

There is no one model or tool kit that says how to be a successful leader... the education needed is in self-awareness.
Binney, Wilke and Williams

Whenever there's a paradox, there's an opportunity to explore both sides of the equation – the 'and... and', rather than 'either... or'. Being real as an enlightened leader is about knowing that you are a being of infinite potential, at the same time as being comfortable with how you are manifesting that potential in the here and now of the physical realm. It's not about setting out to be a saint, and at the same time it is about being a role model. It's not about being perfect, and at the same time it is about being the best you can be – while accepting the limitations of your own human-ness. Being real is about embracing your own personal journey, being loving towards, and forgiving of, yourself and others, and being true to your own values and strengths while giving others the freedom to express theirs. It means:

- Knowing your own strengths and weaknesses in order to surround yourself with people who complement you
- Having the conviction of your own beliefs, and staying true to your values
- Knowing when to say 'no'
- Following through on your public brand – how you should behave based on what you say you believe, and what others believe about you
- Being willing to be vulnerable, comfortable with not having the answers and able to put your hand up and say 'I got it wrong'.
- Facing your fears and taking action anyway
- Being strong in the face of adversity while demonstrating compassion and empathy
- Having confidence in yourself; not hiding behind false modesty but being willing to step out into the light when needed

In essence, authentic leadership is all about *being who you are*, in the midst of doing what you do. In her excellent article for Forbes magazine, Margie Warrell writes 'When all we do is try to fit in, we negate the difference that our difference makes.' But what happens when you're not sure what your difference is?

I recommend starting with your values – your personal values shape the way you think, the way you make decisions and the way you see the world. If you don't know what your top three to five values are, then you are limited in the way in which you can test your own authenticity. Likewise, you need to know what your strengths and talents are – your unique combination of skills and qualities. Don't fool yourself into doing something that frankly someone else could do better. I often joke about my numeric dyslexia, but it is a fact that numbers are simply not my thing. Nor, frankly, is teamwork. I've never been into team sports, not even as a child, and while I love collaborating with people, I am in essence somebody who prefers to work primarily by myself and occasionally to collaborate, rather than be a full-time member of a team. Being real is simply being honest about what you're great and not so great at – and then making sure that your work–life choices support the highest expression of that.

> *With the realisation of one's own potential and self-confidence in one's ability, one can build a better world… That sort of confidence is not a blind one; it is an awareness of one's own potential. On that basis, human beings can transform themselves by increasing the good qualities and reducing negative qualities.*
> Dalai Lama

Part of the difficulty with confidence is that we have a fear it could be interpreted as arrogance. Let's face it, we've all dealt with people whose confidence tipped over into being arrogant. The difference? Arrogance is where your confidence is out of step with reality. If arrogance is at one end of the spectrum, authenticity is at the other. When you're authentic, your confidence is humble. When you're not, it's more likely to be interpreted as fake.

The following questions will help you evaluate how authentic and real you are being as a leader today.

Answer the following on a scale of 1–4: 1 = Not at all, 2 = Sometimes, 3 = Most of the time, 4 = Always

- I consistently lead in alignment with my values
- I consciously use my strengths in my work
- I compensate for my weak areas by delegating to others and/or asking for help
- I go easy on myself when I make mistakes or get it wrong
- I am demanding and expect the best from others, but am forgiving of mistakes
- I am good at saying 'no', and turning down or rejecting others' ideas or work when necessary
- When there is a potential disagreement or conflict I deal with it directly, and with love
- Others perceive me to be an authentic leader (true to my stated values and beliefs)
- Others perceive me to be a leader with integrity (true to my word and promises)
- I can confidently say what my talents are without false modesty or arrogance

Look at the points you answered with a 1 or a 2 and look ahead to specific opportunities you have in the near future to make a shift. It's often a case of bringing awareness to a particular situation, and then evaluating what you did differently that worked, and what could have worked even better.

Authenticity leads to credibility, which according to Stephen M.R. Covey (the late Stephen R. Covey's son) is one of the cornerstones of trust. The era of winging it and 'fake it to make it' is well and truly over. Customers are demanding transparency, and employees are no longer willing, or even able, to follow blindly where you lead. By looking carefully at where you are congruent, where you are leading with integrity, and catching those moments where you may find yourself being less than authentic, presence will naturally follow. ◆

◇◇◇◇◇◇◇◇◇◇◇◇◇◇◇◇◇◇◇◇◇◇◇◇◇◇ **IN A NUTSHELL** ◇◇◇◇◇◇◇◇◇◇◇◇◇◇◇◇◇◇◇◇◇◇◇◇◇◇

1 | Regardless of whether we consider ourselves 'spiritual' or not, most of us are brought up within a moral framework that means we equate being loved with being good and doing well. This sometimes gets in the way of being 'real'.

2 | Authenticity is living in accordance with your values, and playing to your strengths while compensating (in the right way) for your weaknesses.

3 | Be confident in your own abilities and what you know to be true about yourself. You can be confident and humble – in contrast to being arrogant, which is full of self-importance.

◇◇

10

MINDFULNESS – REDUCE STRESS

From time to time, to remind ourselves to relax and be peaceful, we may wish to set aside some time for a retreat, a day of mindfulness, when we can walk slowly, smile, drink tea with a friend, enjoy being together as if we are the happiest people on Earth.

THICH NHAT HANH

From what I see with the clients I work with, and hear from conversations at various networking and business-related events, time (lack of) and the pressure of how much needs to be squeezed into each and every hour is the single biggest challenge for most leaders today. But lack of time isn't the issue – time is actually abundant. It's the amount we try to pack into it that is the problem. Too often, it's the diary and the packed calendars that are managing us, rather than the other way around.

The success of one's life depends on one's ability to forget what is not relevant to the present moment.
Amma

While we've got one eye on the future – the vision and the direction in which we're headed – all of our attention is split between multiple challenges, priorities, tasks and appointments in the present. The result is a high level of workplace sickness and stress, poor performance, an increase in the number of bullying cases, and absenteeism. Even if you're not 'sick', even if you're in fact fully engaged with your work and are inspired by the direction it's heading in, chances are you could be a lot more productive. Typical symptoms of average productivity are overloaded email inboxes, failure to anticipate and address challenges until they need urgent attention, lack of time to invest in relationships, missed opportunities for coaching conversations that could help others' performance and no time allowed for relevant reading to stay on top of industry and business development.

Mindfulness is a practice, as well as a state of being (being mindful). As a practice it is core to many spiritual traditions and is sometimes known by different names, for example 'contemplation', 'meditation' etc., although it in no way requires any religious belief. Companies such as Google, Yahoo, Innocent, Astra Zeneca and Reuters all include mindfulness as part of an employee well-being programme, and it was even introduced as a session at the World Economic Forum in Davos in 2013. Ashridge Business School conducted a mindfulness study in 2011 that showed 90 per cent of participants in the group who meditated each day (Group 1) noted benefits from having participated in the mindfulness activities, 61 per cent noted 'feeling calm', 30 per cent listed 'enjoyed leaving everything and having time to themselves', and 22 per cent also cited 'having a different perspective'. By comparison, only 52 per cent of the group who performed activities other than meditation (Group 2) noted beneficial value from their self-chosen non-meditation activities (e.g. exercise, knitting).

It is also forming a core part of many leadership programmes – the Harvard Business School Faculty member Bill George writes:

The practice of mindful leadership gives you tools to measure and manage your life as you're living it. It teaches you to pay attention to the present moment, recognizing your feelings and emotions and keeping them under control, especially when faced with highly stressful situations. When you are mindful, you're aware of your presence and the ways you impact other people. You're able to both observe and participate in each moment, while recognizing the implications of your actions for the longer term.

It's not exactly a recent phenomenon either. Transport for London (TfL) has been running a mindfulness-based programme since 1979, aimed at reducing stress and improving well-being, and increasing staff resilience under stressful conditions. According to a case study in *Management Today* in 2012:

> *TFL is proud of the results: among those who did the two hours a week, six-week package, days off for stress, anxiety and depression dropped by 71% over the next three years. Attendees reported remarkable improvements in their relationships, sleep and ability to relax.*

So as you're juggling your many priorities, your project plans, your meetings and deadlines, just how do you achieve this state of nirvana – of being fully aware and responsive to each moment in the present? I recommend any or all of the following ten tools that can help:

- Take a minimum of 15 minutes at the start of everyday to take a step back and look at the day ahead of you. What would make this day great? What could get in the way of that, and is there anything you can do about it now? Where do you feel pushed for time, and can you finish one meeting five minutes earlier or start another five minutes later to allow some breathing space?
- Schedule space between meetings. Rushing between meetings means you have no time to properly assess one before the next, nor reflect and make appropriate choices as a result.
- Pay attention to your biorhythms – when you're at your most and least productive – and try to schedule your day accordingly by separating different activities (for example, big-picture creative work, small and short tasks, project work etc.).
- If you're leading a meeting, start with just a few moments quiet to allow people to properly arrive and still the unfocused chatter.
- Between meetings, take at least a two-minute break to centre yourself

and transition from one to the next. My favourite technique for this is from the Buddhist monk Thich Nhat Hanh:

Breathing in, I am calm.
Breathing out, I smile.
Breathing in, present moment.
Breathing out, wonderful moment.

- When you do need to devote your time to future planning and thinking, do it as a conscious activity – rather than letting your thoughts drift towards it in an undisciplined way.
- Learn and practice breathing techniques. How we breathe is directly related to the way our brain works: if our mind is agitated the breath is irregular. If we learn to breathe steadily and deeply, it will not only give us more energy (oxygen), it will also help steady our mind.
- Smile! Research has shown that the phrase 'grin and bear it' may have more truth to it than was intended. A study has shown that if people hold a chopstick or pencil between their teeth – in effect forcing them to smile, then it decreases the heart rate. *Psychology Today* reported: 'Overall researchers believe the findings show that smiling during brief stressors can help to reduce the intensity of the body's stress response, regardless of whether a person actually feels happy.' Reduced stress means the body–mind is more receptive to mindfulness practice.
- When you finish for the day, consciously turn off your mail and internet connection. You are literally shutting down, and giving yourself permission to relax. Look ahead to the next day and make sure what you have in the diary, together with what's on your task list, are actually doable. Stress is partly caused by cramming too much in, and not achieving what you want to over a given period of time.

- Enrol on a beginner's meditation course, and/or a movement practice – martial arts, yoga or dance. I can't recommend it highly enough. It releases tension, creates space in your body that is then reflected in your life, leads to a sense of lightness and gives perspective. My friend and colleague Mark Walsh, founder of Integration Training, runs a great website full of resources that will help you with centring and breathing techniques, all leading to increased mindfulness – go to www.embodied-operatingsystem.com – there's a wealth of accessible video and articles.

When you're leading from purpose, the purpose is greater than your day-to-day concerns. And yet all of us can get weighed down with the multitude of demands on our time. Mindfulness is not just a practice for 15, 20 or 60 minutes a day. It's a moment-to-moment experience, of being rooted in who you are, your own purpose and how it relates to the organisation; in how you relate to others and they to you; and, ultimately, in being at peace – with yourself, with your work and with the world. ◆

◇◇◇◇◇◇◇◇◇◇◇◇◇◇◇◇◇◇◇◇◇◇◇◇◇◇ **IN A NUTSHELL** ◇◇◇◇◇◇◇◇◇◇◇◇◇◇◇◇◇◇◇◇◇◇◇◇◇◇◇◇

1 | It's hard to be present when we have unrealistic demands on our time. Time is actually abundant, but we fill it with too much. Be realistic about what you can achieve, and bring your full attention to each activity.

2 | Mindfulness and meditation practices have been introduced into many business environments with results showing reduced stress, anxiety and depression, and improved relationships.

3 | Breathing techniques, smiling, creating space between meetings and proper planning all facilitate mindfulness and the ability to bring yourself fully to the present.

◇◇

11

INSPIRATION – GET CREATIVE

Like water flowing from an underground spring, human creativity is the wellspring greening the desert of toil and effort, and much of what stifles us in the workplace is the immense unconscious effort on the part of individuals and organisations alike to dam its flow.

DAVID WHYTE, THE HEART AROUSED

Inspiration has long been deemed the domain of the soul. When we are inspired there's a 'fire in our belly', our eyes shine, a surge of happiness flows through our veins and we are connected – connected to that 'something' that is bigger than ourselves, and to the wider universe. Creativity is born of inspiration – it's the external expression of what we care about.

For many people creativity is seen as synonymous with 'art'. Pablo Picasso once said 'All children are artists. The problem is how to remain artists once we grow up.' Think about it – toddlers and children have no qualms about drawing a squiggly line with a few blobs of colour and proudly bringing it home, expecting mum and dad to frame it and put it on the wall as a masterpiece. Sadly, as we grow up and become self-conscious and fearful of judgement, our critic voice tells us that we're not artists – which somehow translates into 'I'm not creative.'

Yet creativity is an innate quality. Sure, some people are naturally more artistic than others, but even if you can't draw, paint, write or compose music, you still have your imagination.

As Sir Ken Robinson says in his seminal TED talk 'How Schools Kill Creativity', creativity is as important as literacy. Unfortunately, most education systems prioritise academic over creative ability, which means 'we don't grow into creativity, we grow out of it'. This is a profound mistake

– an education system that was largely developed in response to the needs of the industrial revolution is no longer serving us today.

In a corporate world where systems, process, compliance and targets shape most people's everyday work experience, there appears to be little room for inspiration and creativity. Yet at the same time 'innovation' is deemed the holy grail of great and successful companies – think Apple and Google. The quest for competitive edge by doing things differently – better and smarter – is a real challenge for most business leaders; but there is precious little space and time allowed for the creative process, for staff to connect to what inspires them and to allow that to emerge in a way that is relevant to the business.

David Whyte, the 'corporate poet' of America whose work inspired me many moons ago to fully embrace my own calling, writes in *The Heart Aroused*:

If these corporate bodies can demand those creative qualities that by long tradition belong so directly to our being, to our soul, they must naturally make room for the soul's disturbing presence within their buildings and borders.

Because the soul can be unpredictable and messy. It doesn't comply with processes and systems – the soul is by its very nature free – which can be quite scary for a lot of managers and leaders to deal with. It's like letting the genie out of the bottle and worrying whether or not it will ever go back in again. What the workplace requires at this time is leaders who are comfortable working with the soul, the heart and the mind as unified coexisting parts of the whole. That's part of presence – the ability to inspire and be inspired, to translate inspiration into creativity that adds value to the business and to still manage the day-to-day reality of what is, not just what could be.

So how can you as a leader embrace inspiration and creativity and foster an environment that allows creativity to emerge? In my experience, it's about creating opportunities for it to happen in a spontaneous manner, while also providing structured forums and space for creative thinking.

I worked for a while with Roland UK – the electronic musical instruments manufacturer with a pretty impressive client list. In between some fairly heavy sessions looking at data and process, these wannabe rock and music stars would go into the musical break room and let rip on the latest keyboards and drums. It was a great form of release for them, and it kept them connected to their passion, the reason they loved working for the company. Granted, it's more difficult to imagine a bunch of young financial advisors getting excited about a break room full of financial product literature to read through in their break. But what would get them excited? A writing wall full of real-life stories of people they'd helped through a stressful time? A monthly challenge to see who could come up with the next evolution of microfinance, or a solution to compete, or even engage, with crowdfunding?

It's also about allowing individual creativity to shine. I'll never forget a Christmas dinner with a client, where the finance director launched into the most beautiful rendition of 'I'm Dreaming of a White Christmas'. It turned out that between the twelve or so people at the table, five or six could create a fabulous choir, and one or two could play instruments (one member of the team was a big swing band player). Music was what connected them – and even those that didn't sing or play an instrument were still connected by the shared memories of music. I wonder whether walls could be created for haiku poems, or paintings and drawings by members of staff where they could be either loaned out or auctioned for charity. These ideas are so simple to implement – they just take a little time and effort to get off the ground.

Then there's the more structured approach to generating innovation from within the company. This is about consulting with your customers, stakeholders and staff about what's working, what's not working and what could be done differently. Large world café facilitation – in which small groups move around the room answering questions on different areas of the business – works well for this. It's about recognising the power of collective intelligence within the organisation, while at the same time looking beyond your own industry to what is being done elsewhere, finding the parallels and then applying the principles where they fit.

Professor Muhammad Yunus, who won a Nobel Peace Prize for spreading the concept of microcredit, has a beautiful story of working with Danone to create a more nutritious yoghurt for Bangladeshi children. Danone created the yogurt but delivered it in a plastic container. Yunus said, 'Plastic isn't allowed. We want biodegradable.' To which the Danone guys protested that they use plastic all over the world. Yunus insisted, and they came back with an edible cup. As he says 'These big companies have enormous creative power. But unless you ask, you'll never get an answer.'

And what about you? Challenge yourself. What are you doing that is simply 'the way it's always been done', versus what could really make a difference – not just to your own customers, but to the wider community and planet? How can you stay inspired and able to tap into your own creativity? To be present means to feel fully alive, connected and tapped into whatever it is that drives you – your beliefs, your passions and your sense of purpose. Stay inspired by staying connected to that. Create space in your diary to reflect, to take walks, even to cloud-gaze. Cultivate your ability to daydream, to connect the dots, to see how ideas can relate to each other and create new ways of looking at a problem. We often have the dots but rarely the whole picture. The whole picture comes when we step back far enough to see it, when we are able to see the space between the dots and have the imagination to fill that space with whatever wants to emerge in the moment. Creativity happens in a moment, and you have to be ready for those moments – aware and available. ◆

1 | Creativity is a product of inspiration – it has nothing to do with whether you are 'artistic' or not.

2 | Innovation is a known competitive differentiator – the 'holy grail' of many businesses. But the right conditions are needed to foster it – structured and unstructured approaches are needed for it to be generated.

3 | Stay inspired. Being present means regularly connecting to and following what inspires you. Allow room for your imagination to play, to ask 'what if?' and to look for patterns that you hadn't noticed before.

◇◇

12

JOY – BE HAPPY

Where there is the Infinite there is joy... Only in the infinite there is joy: know the nature of the Infinite.

THE UPANISHADS

Everyone, deep down, wants to be happy. It's a key driver across all of humankind, and all cultures. The challenge is that different people need different things to make them happy; it's a subjective experience and can also be quite transitory. So measuring it is very difficult.

According to the Eastern spiritual traditions, the overarching philosophy is that the source of our unhappiness comes from being attached and over-reliant on the external material world – which can change in a heartbeat – rather than identifying with the infinite never-ending stream of consciousness that is beyond form, and of which we form a part.

You are not just a drop in the ocean, you are also the ocean in the drop.
Rumi

Happiness and success are closely related. As Robert Holden, a leading researcher and writer on happiness and success intelligence, writes, 'We do not become happy because we are successful; we become successful because we are happy.' The two are inextricably linked. For some, happiness and success are defined by a job title, a salary grade, by having a loving family and enough time to enjoy the results of hard labour. For others it'll be less about what their life *looks like*, and defined more by how they *feel* – satisfied, fulfilled and a sense of having a higher purpose.

Psychologist Martin Seligman also asserts that happiness is not derived from external, momentary pleasures, and has developed the following acronym to sum up when humans are happiest – PERMA. For each letter I've correlated it to the aspect of happiness that is experienced or expressed as a spiritual quality – contentment, fulfilment, love and purpose.

P *Pleasure:* While this is usually taken to mean the enjoyment of transient experiences such as a good meal or a walk in the park, I think it also follows that in the workplace people get pleasure from giving help to others – of being of service. Deepak Chopra, in answer to the question 'What's the single most important thing that can lead to happiness?', replied, 'Make someone else happy.' Pleasure leads to the aspect of happiness called *contentment* – that sense of 'all being right with the world', albeit often a temporary experience.

E *Engagement:* This point relates to the concept of flow, the absorption of a challenging yet enjoyable activity. Flow is the state that results when you are engaged in an activity or process that seems effortless, where time disappears and where it can feel almost as if something is working through you – that you're not the 'doer' but the channel. For many, this is a sure sign that they are using their skills and talents to the full, and the more often they experience this state, the more likely it is that they are following their 'true path'. This leads to the *fulfilment* aspect of happiness. Experientially, fulfilment is often a sense of having been emptied, of having given one's all, of having gone above and beyond – and yet in the emptiness comes the feeling of fullness, of being fulfilled – spent and used, but in a good way.

R *Relationships:* When I've observed people being at their happiest at work it has more often than not been because they feel secure in their role in the organisation, and because they feel they belong. Many people form long-lasting emotional ties with friends, and even their spouses, through a work setting. *Love* is a core component of happiness. At our core, each of us is longing to love and be loved, and relationships at work fulfil this need for many people.

M *Meaning:* Defined as 'a perceived quest or belonging to something bigger', this comes back to the notion of *purpose* as an aspect of happiness – the giving of one's time and talents in service of something that is considered worthwhile. People are happy when they are contributing to something greater and bigger than themselves.

A *Accomplishments:* We all know how it feels to have accomplished a goal or objective that took commitment, focus and an investment of time and effort. The sense of reward from having achieved it is key to our overall sense of well-being (*fulfilment*), especially within a work context where ultimately everyone wants to feel like they have a contribution to make. That said, this latter aspect of happiness can also be the cause of much unhappiness in the workplace – largely because of the sense of ownership by the person doing the work. This is where ego can really do damage, where identification with the sense of 'I am doing the work' can mean that more assertive, goal-orientated personalities dominate the workplace, tending to overshadow people who perform the support functions, who enable others' success, without blowing their own trumpet.

Whoever does things without personal desire for the results is called wise by the sages.
Sri Swami Satchidananda, The Bhagavad Gita, 3.19

In my own personal experience, doing 'my' work without attachment to the results has been one of the hardest spiritual practices. But the practice in and of itself has really helped me to be happier, going beyond the psychological and emotional aspects of happiness, and allowing me to tap into the deeper aspects that are attained through the spiritual attitude of surrender. Our responsibility is to show up fully and perform our duty to our best, using the talents and gifts that have been given to us. The rest is beyond our control.

While we might attain happiness from temporary moments of pleasure, from accomplishing a goal and engaging in a particular activity, joy is a deeper emotion that is experienced independently of the external world, and is derived from a much deeper place of knowing that 'all is well' and connecting to the present moment and all it has to offer.

There is a world of difference between the pursuit of happiness and following your joy. The pursuit of happiness turns life into a race, it dismisses inner joy, encourages destination addiction, and confuses success with sacrifice. Following your joy lets your innate happiness teach you what you really value and what your true purpose is. People who follow their joy discover a depth of creativity and talent that inspires the world. They are assisted by grace and inspiration to contribute to the collective wealth of mankind. Their joy is their compass that navigates them through the tough times.
Robert Holden

So, when we pursue happiness we tend to seek it in the external realm of success, whereas joy is an inner quality that is born of the soul being happy, connected to the infinite supply of abundance and grace that is available to us in each and every moment. That's not to say that we can't pursue material gains – but they come from tapping into joy and allowing our lives to be an expression of it. When you are doing 'worthwhile work', there is a peaceful and joyful acceptance of whatever results.

So what does it take to be a fully present and joyful leader of an enlightened business? Here are my top ten tips to tap into your own joy while creating an environment for others to express theirs:

• *Be generous of yourself.* Don't hide. Give yourself full permission to express yourself fully in your work – all of you, including the whacky bits.

- *Be spontaneous.* Spontaneity is fertiliser for the soul. Do something different, just for the hell of it. Surprise people.
- *Smile.* A smile can convey irrepressible joy and is incredibly infectious.
- *Have fun.* Play a game, do something different. Dance it. Tell a joke. Look at the funny side of things. Start a meeting by asking someone to share the funniest story they've ever heard.
- *Be optimistic.* The more we focus on what's wrong, the more difficult it is to tap into joy. There is wisdom in those immortal Monty Python lyrics, 'always look on the bright side of life' (yes go on, hum the tune).
- *Celebrate.* Heading straight for the bar is the more usual way to celebrate. But there are other ways – telling and sharing stories, creating a memory board etc.
- *Allow healthy difference of opinions.* Joy comes from acknowledging differences and appreciating paradox rather than struggling against it. Holding the discomfort of conflict while appreciating our differences can be joyful in its own way.
- *Break old habits* (rather than living a life of habit). Joy is stifled by routine because we lose our ability to be present. When we are in the unknown we are called to be present and more aware of the choices we are making.
- *Make conscious choices.* Pay attention to what you are saying 'yes' to. We are much more accustomed to saying 'yes' than 'no' – practise both and watch where you are putting your attention. Is it leading you to joy or away from it?
- *Give others permission to be their glorious selves.* It's hard enough to give ourselves full permission to be our fullest glorious selves, so it's a real gift when we can give it to others. Ask them what they really think, how they truly feel. Invite them to drop the mask. Make it safe for them to do so.

Create space for happiness and joy, and the way you and others experience work and business will transform the results. ◆

1 | Happiness is derived from external pleasure, joy from within.

2 | Martin Seligman's acronym PERMA (pleasure, engagement, relationships, meaning and accomplishments) sums up the different sources of joy and happiness.

3 | Success and happiness are interlinked. Create an environment that leads to joy – for yourself and others. Spontaneity, fun and optimism are all important for a fun and joy-full workplace.

◇◇

13

COMPASSION – KINDNESS AT WORK

It doesn't interest me what planets are squaring your moon;
I want to know if you have touched the centre of your own sorrow, if you
have been opened by life's betrayals or have become shrivelled and closed
from fear of further pain.

I want to know if you can sit with pain, mine or your own, without
moving to hide it, or fade it or fix it.
I want to know if you can see beauty even when it is not pretty every day,
if you can source your life from its presence.

ORIAH MOUNTAIN DREAMER

Most organisations I have worked with have at least one value that expresses the notion of innovation, another the need for teamwork, and another the quality of delivery or customer service. Some may have a value of respect. But what about love, kindness and compassion? What value heading would they fit under, and why do they matter?

All of the world's spiritual traditions teach compassion, often referred to as 'love in action'. We often feel overwhelmed when faced with natural disasters or catastrophes abroad, or the incomprehensible ravages of war affecting populations remote and removed from our own backyards. The fact is that right where we live and work, there are people who need our help and support.

Being present means being able to live with the knowledge that, on one level at least, all is exactly as it should be – to have an acceptance of the circumstances in which we and others find ourselves. However, that doesn't mean that we should ignore the pain of others. My teacher Amma, who has been travelling the world and consoling people of all nationalities for the last

30 years, has said that physical and material poverty will only be eradicated when the poverty of our hearts has been healed, when we are able to open our hearts to others' suffering and take action to help.

Presence means having the capacity to hold one's own joy and happiness while sitting with another's pain. It's easy, as I did for many years, to live in a Pollyanna world and believe that everything is rosy and light, perfect and according to God's will. My rose-coloured glasses prevented me from facing up to the fact that for many people life is a daily struggle. My personal wake-up call came when I found myself at the heart of the 2004 tsunami in South India. Homes were destroyed, children lost their parents and families lost their only means of income. Witnessing the destruction, grief and pain of loss on such a large scale was overwhelming. It affected me on a profound level and finally woke me up to the harsh reality that is life for many on this planet.

In business, empathy is a word that is more often used than compassion. The two are, however, different – empathy being the ability to share and understand someone's pain without necessarily wanting to do anything about it, while compassion involves the extra step of wanting to reach out and help.

Research is showing that the action of helping others in the workplace produces a higher state of well-being, the so-called virtuous cycle that translates into higher productivity and engagement, better customer service, and less stress-induced leave and the associated health care costs. Psychologist Jonathan Haidt, at the New York University Stern School of Business, calls the resulting feeling of compassion 'elevation' – 'a warm, uplifting feeling that people experience when they experience unexpected acts of human goodness, kindness, courage or compassion. It makes a person want to help others and to become a better person himself or herself.' Emma Seppala at the Center for Compassion and Altruism and Research at Stanford backs this up in an article in *Psychology Today*. When employees experience 'elevation' they *are more willing to help peers and to provide customer service on their own accord. What's more, compassionate, friendly, and supportive co-workers tend to build higher-quality relationships with others at work. In doing so, they boost co-workers' productivity levels and increase co-workers' feelings of social connection, as well as their commitment to the workplace and their levels of engagement with their job.*

Rather than feeling powerless to help and despondent about the scale of need, small actions add up and do make a difference at a local level.

In his excellent book, *Please Take One* - *One Step Towards a More Generous Life,* Mike Dickson tells the story of the starfish to illustrate this point.

A man was walking along a beach. The sun was shining and it was a beautiful day. In the distance he could see a young boy going back and forth between the surf's edge and the beach. Then he noticed hundreds of starfish stranded on the sand. The boy was hurling them one by one back into the sea.

The man was struck by the apparent futility of the task. There were far too many starfish to save. But as he approached, the boy continued picking up starfish one by one and throwing them into the surf.

'You must be crazy', said the man when he reached him. 'There are thousands of miles of beach covered in starfish. You can't possibly make a difference.' The boy held the man's gaze. He then stooped down, picked up one more starfish and threw it back into the ocean. He turned back to the man and smiled. 'It made a difference to that one!'

When it comes to compassion in the workplace, I have seen many examples of teams rallying around a colleague who is experiencing a difficult time, through cancer or other disease, bereavement or emotional trauma. When we witness someone who we are close to go through pain and hardship, it evokes the compassion inside of us, the natural instinct to want to comfort and help in any way possible. It's easier when it's people we know.

It's also easier when the difficulty is one we can relate to. We can appreciate that losing a loved one or going through cancer treatment is hard – we can grasp the context of the situation and relate to the difficulty. But what happens to our compassion when the illness or trauma is hidden, and not so easy to identify?

Emotional and mental illness is a very real problem in business today. According to the Shaw Trust, which aims to tackle the last workplace taboo, not managing mental illness at work is costing UK employers 'over £26bn a year. We therefore literally cannot afford to neglect this problem any longer'. Sufferers will often find it hard to be stable, may erupt in anger from time to time and suffer from bouts of depression that affect their mood. It's a challenge when a company is wanting to live by values and set a standard for acceptable behaviour, to also be compassionate with individuals who do have the aptitude and skills for the job, and who *on the whole* perform well, but who occasionally are unable to behave in a way that is congruent and consistent with the company ethos.

Emma Vernon, Human Resources Business Partner at a client who has received Gold level Investors in People accreditation, has experience working with people needing additional support, and together with the HR team has created an environment that allows them to thrive and flourish. She has told me:

I think people see the integrity behind our compassion; that it's not a token gesture. We have a genuine interest in the well-being of our employees, which I believe partly stems from the feeling that one day you could be 'in their shoes' and you would hope that you too would be considered with respect and care.

How can organisations demonstrate compassion? Here are a few ideas to get started:

- *Reward random acts of kindness.* A client recently gave a 'Superhero award' to an employee who had spontaneously sent a customer a get well card on hearing they were ill.
- *Promote the 'human' side of HR.* Ensure there is at least one person available who can provide a sympathetic listening ear at any time.
- *Don't 'sweep things under the carpet'.* If an employee is going through tough times, ensure there is space for colleagues to discuss the impact at both a day-to-day task and emotional level. Colleagues will often feel stressed and conflicted when supporting a colleague – the pressure of their own jobs as well as taking on the additional workload, together with the emotional stress, can sometimes be a lot to deal with.
- *Foster a safe environment.* This is where people can ask for help when needed. Being overwhelmed and fear of job security can often prevent people from saying 'I can't cope' – leading to breakdowns that then impact on customers and relationships at work.

Balancing the rational and cognitive aspects of work with the relational, emotional aspects of working in a community with others is one of the biggest challenges for leaders, and indeed everyone working in business today. Reflect on how kindness and compassion can be part of your leadership presence; there is no shortage of opportunities to practise these timeless spiritual qualities.

> *This is my simple religion. There is no need for temples; no need for complicated philosophy. Our own brain, our own heart is our temple; the philosophy is kindness… Be kind whenever possible. It is always possible.*
> Dalai Lama

1 | Helping others leads to a higher state of well-being and a more supportive working environment. It can also lead to higher productivity and customer service.

2 | Compassion is important not just for recognisable life challenges such as cancer or bereavement, but also for hidden or less well understood conditions such as depression and mental illness.

3 | Consider what value heading compassion, care and kindness fit under in your organisation. How is it recognised and rewarded?

◇◇

14

GRATITUDE - SHOW APPRECIATION

People deal too much with the negative, with what is wrong… Why not try
and see positive things, to just touch those things and make them bloom?

THICH NHAT HANH

In the same way that joy is the deeper, inner quality that leads to happiness, so gratitude is the quality that needs to be deeply felt in order for thankfulness and appreciation to be expressed. Happy, productive organisations are fuelled by gratitude and appreciation – it's hard to imagine a workplace that nurtures people's talents and creativity if it's a cesspit of criticism, non-stop moaning and finger pointing. And yet how many organisations truly look to create a culture of gratitude and appreciation at their core?

As a leader of an enlightened business, team or organisation, it's important to tap into gratitude on a daily basis in order for it to be reflected in your working environment. Primarily, it's a mindset. We may have been conditioned through our education system and the relentless onslaught of marketing messages that we're not good enough, that we should always strive for more, and that perfection is a state somewhere off in the future. The spiritual truth, however, is that everything is perfect exactly as it is, and that if we can be grateful for our lives, the people in them and the gifts that are available to us on a daily basis, so our experience of it improves – along with that of our co-workers and teams.

So how to cultivate an attitude of gratitude so that it becomes a daily practice? The most popular and by all accounts very effective way is to start a 'gratitude journal', a weekly or biweekly practice to reflect on and write down what you are grateful for, and to truly be aware of the gifts in your life. Robert A. Emmons, the world's leading scientific expert on gratitude, recommends the following to get the most out of the practice:

- *Don't just go through the motions.* Research suggests that journaling is more effective if you first make the conscious decision to become happier and more grateful.
- *Go for depth over breadth.* Elaborating in detail about a particular thing for which you're grateful carries more benefits than a superficial list of many things.
- *Get personal.* Focusing on *people* to whom you are grateful has more of an impact than focusing on *things* for which you are grateful.
- *Try subtraction, not just addition.* One effective way of stimulating gratitude is to reflect on what your life would be like *without* certain blessings, rather than just tallying up all those good things.
- *Savour surprises.* Try to record events that were unexpected or surprising, as these tend to elicit stronger levels of gratitude.
- *Don't overdo it.* Writing occasionally (once or twice per week) is more beneficial than daily journaling.

In the physical, dualistic world, it can be difficult to see things as perfect when deadlines are being missed, products aren't selling as well as hoped or star performers leave to join the competition. It's not about denial of what is, but rather a rebalancing and maintaining of perspective in terms of appreciating the small things in life, while dealing with everyday challenges.

One kind word can warm three winter months.
Japanese proverb

How does a deep feeling of gratitude translate into a culture of appreciation and thankfulness in the workplace? Obviously, saying a sincere thank you is a good place to start. In a survey of 2000 Americans by the John

Templeton Foundation in 2013, people were less likely to feel or express gratitude at work than anywhere else. One theory is that work is fundamentally an economic exchange, rather than something done out of the goodness of people's hearts. Yet, according to data gathered from the gratitude website run by the Greater Good Science Centre, expressing gratitude leads to a sense of self-worth, self-efficacy and trust between employees.

So how can gratitude be expressed in a meaningful way, in a way that will be warmly received and welcomed?

A client of mine is exceptionally good at this. Aside from regular awards for those who really go above and beyond to embody the company values, thank you cards are available to team leaders and managers to use as and when they're merited. One manager came up with the idea of a 'pay it forward' scheme, under which team leaders and managers could have a discretionary spend for cinema tickets, gift vouchers, chocolates – small gifts that reflect the care and time taken in the selection and purchase of the gift, rather than a perfunctory thank you. Following an off-site strategy meeting I facilitated for the leadership team I received a beautiful bouquet of flowers, and I can say hand on heart that a gesture of thanks works – the sense of value and appreciation is immense. However, I would caution you to retain an element of surprise. If it becomes a process and loses its spontaneity then the impact is diminished – say thank you whenever and wherever possible, but keep the gifts ad hoc and random.

Appreciation is a wonderful thing. It makes what is excellent in others belong to us as well.
Voltaire

Traditionally, management has looked at improving the business by looking at what's wrong, defining the problem and looking at how to solve it. Increasingly, the practice of appreciative enquiry is taking over as a strength-based approach to building a business. Similar to the theory that it's more productive to develop your existing skills than focus on improving weaker areas, appreciative enquiry takes its starting point from what's working in the organisation, and then looks at how to build on that.

Table 2 | A Comparison of Problem Solving and Appreciative Enquiry

Problem Solving	Appreciative Enquiry
Felt need, identification of problem(s)	Appreciating, valuing the best of what is
Analysis of causes	Envisioning what might be
Analysis of possible solutions	Engaging in dialogue about what should be
Action planning	Innovating, creating what will be

It may seem to be a subtle difference, but starting from a place of gratitude and appreciation for what is working means that there can be a more sustainable, generative process of incremental improvement, which in turn runs less risk of wholesale change programmes that can emerge from the problem-solving approach. In addition, if there is a strong sense that things are going well, it can psychologically help people to feel that they're part of something that works, rather than something that is broken.

I used this approach with the aforementioned client, at the beginning of a new phase of their development from entrepreneurial start-up to fast-growing medium-sized company. There was a natural fear that the company would lose the very spirit that had shaped it to be the successful business it had become, and the very first thing we did was to look at 'what had got them here', and what was intrinsic to their success. The outputs from this session then shaped the values and communications across the company, so that in parallel with the necessary organisational and process changes, people could see that it was holding on to what was important, and allowing that to shape the company's vision for the future.

Effective leadership of others starts with rigorous leadership of self. Not just in terms of time management, staying on top of industry developments, networking and the like, but in terms of the essential qualities that determine your character. These in turn shape how people will relate to you, how they talk about you and how successful you can be as a business leader and inspirational role model. Commitment, authenticity, mindfulness, inspiration, joy, compassion and gratitude are fundamental qualities for leaders to bring to business today. Some days they are easier to tap into than others, but if you regularly review and assess the extent to which you've been able to embody and bring them into your work, you'll see and feel the difference, and those you work with will too. ◆

◇◇◇◇◇◇◇◇◇◇◇◇◇◇◇◇◇◇◇◇◇◇◇◇◇◇◇ IN A NUTSHELL ◇◇◇◇◇◇◇◇◇◇◇◇◇◇◇◇◇◇◇◇◇◇◇◇◇◇◇◇

1 | Happy, productive workplaces are fuelled by genuine appreciation. Gratitude is the quality that makes appreciation genuine and heartfelt.

2 | Create a culture of appreciation. Opportunities for managers to say 'thank you' in a personalised way, awards, a 'wall of fame' and promoting stories on an intranet all help contribute to an organisation that values its people rather than just pays lip-service.

3 | The process of appreciative enquiry looks at how to grow by building on strengths, imagining what's possible and innovating accordingly, rather than taking a problem-solving approach. It's a subtle but powerful difference.

◇◇

THREE

◇◇◇◇◇◇◇◇◇◇◇◇◇◇◇◇◇◇◇

LEADING INTO POTENTIAL

*For the wise man looks into space and he knows
there is no limited dimension.*

LAO TZU

◆

15

COMMUNITY – FIND YOUR TRIBE

We know ourselves as individuals but only because we live in community.
Love, trust, fellowship, selflessness are all mediated to us through our
interdependence… We are individually free but also communally bound.
We cannot act without affecting others and others cannot act without
affecting us. We know ourselves as we are reflected in the faces,
action and attitudes of each other.

JANET SCOTT

While the spiritual journey is in essence an individual one, defined by the personal relationship we have with spirit, God, love or however we define it, across the world and in all cultures the notion of community is at the core of how people come together in celebration of their faith and beliefs, to share their joys and sorrows and to connect to those with whom they share a natural affinity. The Merriam-Webster dictionary defines community as 'a social, religious, occupational or other group sharing common characteristics or interests and perceived or perceiving itself as distinct in some respect from the larger society within which it exists'.

If we consider the traits of community in the spiritual sense, many of these same traits apply equally to the business world. There is a common purpose and shared beliefs; people know each other well and care for each other; there is joy – fun and laughter; there is a sense of service; and there is (usually) a hierarchical structure.

Community, however, isn't just limited to a group of people who self-identify with a particular belief system or purpose. As a business leader knows, an organisation forms part of a wider ecosystem – the company touches not just the lives of those working in it, but those of its suppliers, customers and competitors. Yet while any director will intellectually know this, how many businesses demonstrate this awareness – truly? As long as we are still trapped in the paradigm of 'self' and 'others', it will be difficult to bring the true essence of community to life.

In some organisations, community is confused with the notion of family. I don't mean family-run businesses, but the sense that 'we're a family'. Netflix's CEO, Reed Hastings, in one famous presentation on his company's culture said 'We're a team, not a family.' If you think about it, in most cases a family has no option but to tolerate bad behaviour and dysfunctional relationships. But this isn't the case in the business world – despite how often it happens. Employment and client contracts govern expectations on both sides in terms of the exchange of talent, goods and services in return for financial compensation. Therefore, work is primarily a transactional business relationship.

This makes the community side of business all the more important – driven by an altruistic, human aspect of care; for example, the exchange of specialised skills and resources to charities who in turn provide real-life insights for employees into their customers' challenges.

But the term community doesn't necessarily mean 'soft'. Companies such as Legal & General, KFC and Anglian Water are taking a much harder look at how to integrate traditional volunteering initiatives with their business strategy. They're doing this by partnering with charities and creating real-life opportunities to put into practice what leaders have learned through training and development programmes – immersive learning. Jan Levy, Managing Director of Three Hands, an organisation that helps businesses work with communities, said in HR Magazine, 'Just creating social value is no longer enough – there has to be business value alongside it.' Coming back to the notion of CSV, Levy prefers the term 'community investment' – the process 'by which companies contribute to a healthier community with a view to making the business healthier'. As an example, frontline staff at Legal & General have been trained by Macmillan Cancer Care to make sure they are suitably sensitive when taking calls relating to critical illness cover. Those in the home insurance business have spent days with the Royal National Lifeboat Institution to better understand flooding issues.

It's not just about giving opportunities for volunteering, it's about gaining first-hand insight into what their customers are experiencing – taking it from the theoretical to the practical and experiential. In other words, broadening the notion of community within the organisation, to include the partnerships that are essential to their success.

John Lewis plc is a long-standing example of how to build community in terms of partnership: the model whereby all employees – regardless of title or tenure – are considered partners in the business and are shareholders by default. Waitrose supermarkets have a programme of community giving that actively engages with customers – nominating local charities or organisations to support online, and receiving a token that represents a £ value of monthly profit to donate to one of three charities of choice every time they shop.

So how will the notion of community evolve? The potential emerging for some time now has been led by Seth Godin, who pioneered the use of the term 'tribe' in the context of connecting people beyond the company or business. In addition to having community spirit, a company can exponentially increase its impact and influence by creating a tribe.

A tribe is a group of people connected to one another, connected to a leader, and connected to an idea. For millions of years, human beings have been part of one tribe or another. A group needs only two things to be a tribe: a shared interest and a way to communicate.
Seth Godin

As Seth says, we are essentially tribal in nature. We want to belong, and we want to hang out with people who see the world the same way we do. With social media and social CRM transforming how businesses communicate and market themselves, knowing who your tribe is – both at an individual leadership level and at a business level – is one of the keys to sustainable success. It means you'll be able to tap into others' ideas and passions, co-create a better future, get instant feedback on product or service development and create a pool of goodwill that exemplifies the wheel of karma – the notion of 'pay it forward'.

If I had to summarise all the scientific literature on the causes of human happiness in one word, that word would be 'social'. We are by far the most social species on Earth. Even ants have nothing on us. If I wanted to predict your happiness, and I could know only one thing about you, I wouldn't want to know your gender, religion, health or income. I'd want to know about your social network – about your friends and family and the strength of your bonds with them.
Harvard Psychology Professor, Daniel Gilbert

So how do you find or even start a tribe? Here are some ideas to get started:

- *Social media.* Absolutely great to meet and connect with people who share the same passions and interests. Find them through keywords, tagging and, most importantly, join the conversation.
- *Networking.* Niche networking is the best way to meet people who are like-minded and have similar interests.
- *Take risks.* You'll never know what's out there unless you're willing to just give it a go. You might find yourself surrounded by a few geeks and nerds for the evening, but other than that what have you really got to lose?
- *Start a movement.* The above are all great to meet and hang out with people who share the same interests. But if your purpose and mission are

exciting enough you'll be able to put out the idea and inspire others to take action around it – it will naturally attract people to you, and before long you'll be leading a tribe.

- *Connect with and to others.* No tribe exists as a stand-alone entity. Be an evangelist for your own ideas and beliefs, while supporting others who are of a similar mindset.

This last one is the central point of being part of, or leading, a tribe. We live in a world that craves to be connected – at a social level and at an ideas level. It is such an exciting time. Two years ago I was privileged to attend the first International Conference on Technology Enhanced Education at Amrita University in Kerala – exploring how distance learning can educate the millions of India's population living below the poverty line. It explored how information and knowledge could be made broadly available via open-source platforms, with skills training delivered via e-learning platforms. For the first time, we have the tools and capability to bridge ideas and populations, and make resources widely available. The huge conglomerates wanting to control the distribution of products and services through patents and unsustainable commercial practices will find themselves alienated by the weight of demand for cheaper and more ethical alternatives. This will only happen through the power of tribes – powerful groups of people, globally connected and determined to make the world a better and more just place to live – for all.

So – where and who is your tribe? How can you extend your existing community to have more influence, create more change and deliver a more lasting impact? What are the connections you need to elevate your networking to be more powerful than just a number of LinkedIn contacts? Think community and tribe, and watch what happens. ◆

1 | Community is an age-old term that defines a group of people bound by shared characteristics and interests. Typically, members of a community all know each other, and are bound by a sense of belonging. Tribe extends this concept beyond geographic constraints to the realm of ideas, and has the power to connect strangers across the world. Vast and unlimited potential lies in being able to connect your mission to a tribe.

2 | CSV is more than CSR, and 'giving back'. It's a virtuous win–win cycle of direct business benefit, where making a difference and leaving a legacy directly supports the company mission.

3 | Start with your own social network – physical and virtual – and make connections to like-minded groups and organisations. Contribute and share, offer your own help and expertise, and ask for feedback. Goodwill and the notion of 'pay it forward' go a long way.

◇◇

16

SEEKING – ASK BETTER QUESTIONS

It is not speech which we should want to know:
we should know the speaker.
It is not things seen which we should want to know:
we should know the seer.
It is not sounds which we should want to know:
we should know the hearer.
It is not mind which we should want to know:
we should know the thinker.

THE UPANISHADS

In the old paradigm of leadership and business, leaders were expected to have all the answers. That was the point – they were promoted based on their experience and expertise, and everyone looked up to them for guidance. That was when the world was relatively more stable, when five-year business plans really did last five years and when few dared to challenge the status quo. Now that's all changed. As a leader today, you have to know what questions to ask, how to look for options, explore scenarios, consult with others and ultimately make decisions and judgement calls based on a mix of experience, data, insight and intuition.

But most of all, you have to know what questions to ask – if you don't start with the right question, how can you hope to get the right answer?

On the spiritual path, one who wants to know the ultimate answers to life – Who am I? Why am I here? What/who is 'God'? – is known as a seeker. There were times many years ago when I thought I would go crazy asking these questions, having no clue how to find the answers. My family and friends can testify to many sessions into the early hours of the morning, going round in endless circles exploring the meaning of life. Ultimately, I found peace through meditation and yoga, although it wasn't until I met my teacher Amma that I was truly able to feel that I had found my way, and to develop the patience to recognise that the answers reveal themselves in time, as and when we are ready to receive them.

A sculptor sees an image to be carved where others find only wood and stone.
A seeker, distinguishing the eternal from the ephemeral, chooses the Everlasting.
Amma

In today's complex world, it is a brave and wise leader indeed who is comfortable with the unknown, able to hold the questions while dedicating the proper amount of time and reflection before rushing to an answer. And yet, the pressure that comes from our fast-paced and changing environment is to make snap decisions based on what is available at the time – pressurised by the need to gain competitive advantage and achieve short-term targets. So how can you balance this need for quick, but informed and well-judged answers? The short answer: ask better questions.

Successful people ask better questions, and as a result, they get better answers.
Tony Robbins

On the basis that many people in your organisation will have at least part of the answer, or at the very least an informed perspective of the answer, the ability to know who to ask – and what questions to ask – is key. One way to practise asking better questions is to learn from journalists. Here are some top journalist tips from Fast Company for asking great questions, followed by my own observations:

- *Don't ramble on – terminate the sentence at the question mark.* Be concise, and don't try to fill in the answer with options you've thought of.

- *Get comfortable with silence.* Allow space for the answer to emerge. This comes back to presence – the ability to simply 'be' with the question.
- *Start with who, what, when, where, how or why for more meaningful answers.* We all know that open questions lead to better answers, but it's amazing how often people unintentionally close off answers.
- *Don't fish for the answer you want.* It comes across as manipulative, you lose credibility and it wastes time. Challenge yourself beforehand to make sure that personal motive is not getting in the way of the 'greater good'.
- *Stop nodding if you don't understand – ask a follow-up question instead.* Have the courage to say 'I'm sorry, I don't understand…', and be comfortable with asking for clarification.
- *If you get a non-answer, approach it again from a different angle.* This relies on the ability to truly listen to the answer that's given. Great listening comes from having an 'empty' mind – that is, free from any preconceived ideas about what the answer will be.
- *Rephrase the answer in your own words.* Simply, check for understanding. Most often called 'active listening', it once again ensures that you are not simply hearing what you want to hear, but truly listening to the answer that is given.
- *Don't be afraid to ask 'dumb' questions.* It's often hard for a leader to say 'I don't know' or 'Please help me understand'. It's also one of the most powerful statements a leader can make, as it helps others step into their own strengths and expertise.

This final point is at the heart of what is needed to create a 'coaching culture'. Sir John Whitmore, credited with being an originator of the Goal-Reality-Options-Will (GROW) model, defines coaching as 'helping someone to get the best performance out of themselves – the potential for which was already there. Coaching is about releasing that potential.' The skill and tools of coaching have been instrumental in transforming the way leadership operates in organisations over the past decade. Used to encourage and support development and achievement of goals, it facilitates thinking and helps coachees to find their own answers rather than relying on what they're told. Developing a coaching culture also leads to greater accountability, and gives people the confidence to ask, 'Why are we doing this?', or 'How can we do this better?'

Leadership transforms individual potential into collective performance.
Fred Kofman

Coming back to the spiritual aspect of seeking and asking better questions – it's about developing the ability to continually look beyond the obvious, to peel back the layers of what's available through the physical senses and look beyond. This is where the power of realising potential lies – with being able to sense what's wanting to emerge, what threats are around the corner or what action to take next. This 'sixth' sense is intuition, the ability to know something instinctively, without the need for conscious reasoning. Developing it requires commitment to stillness, to creative endeavours, to time in nature and, for the more mystical in nature, prayer and reflection. Some entrepreneurs rely exclusively on their intuition to make decisions, while others need to explore every option, research alternatives and have every scenario mapped out with possible outcomes. Neither is right or wrong – the important part is to know which end of the spectrum you tend to inhabit, and then ask questions of others who complement you or who may have a different perspective.

Most importantly, as the pace of change becomes ever faster, it's about being comfortable with the unknown and recognising that whatever answer may appear to be right today, it may no longer apply tomorrow. Having a sense of the immortal, infinite nature of life and the world helps us to tap into our own, others' and the business's potential. At a spiritual, existential level these answers are only available to us through contemplation and dedicated earnest seeking for truth; at a leadership level it comes from being comfortable with asking the right questions and listening for the answers.

I beg you… to have patience with everything unresolved in your heart and try to love the questions themselves as if they were locked rooms or books written in a very foreign language. Don't search for the answers, which could not be given you now, because you would not be able to live them. And the point is, to live everything. Live the questions now. Perhaps then, someday far in the future, you will gradually, without ever noticing it, live your way into the answer…
Maria Rainer Rilke

◇◇◇◇◇◇◇◇◇◇◇◇◇◇◇◇◇◇◇◇◇◇◇◇◇ **IN A NUTSHELL** ◇◇◇◇◇◇◇◇◇◇◇◇◇◇◇◇◇◇◇◇◇◇◇◇◇

1 | Leadership today is more about asking the right questions than having the right answers.

2 | Listening is a critical leadership skill. Listen to what is being said, not being said and why – as well as to your own intuition.

3 | Developing a coaching culture is one of the best ways to ensure that better questions are asked throughout the organisation, and that people are able to navigate unknown territory and respond appropriately.

◇◇

17

CONNECTION – COMMUNICATION AND CONFLICT RESOLUTION

Humankind has not woven the web of life. We are but one thread within it. Whatever we do to the web, we do to ourselves. All things are bound together. All things connect.

CHIEF SEATTLE

Connection is vital to our physical, emotional and spiritual health. Relationships define our working lives – those people we work with and for, inside and outside the organisation. I can't think of a business or organisation of any kind that could survive without relationships, and the lifeblood of relationships is our connection to them. Communication is a vital expression of how and who we connect with at work. And yet, ask any leader what the main cause of conflict and breakdowns of understanding are in their organisation, and the answer is very likely to be poor communication. Time pressures, cultural and language differences, and multiple technology platforms all contribute to failures in our ability to truly connect and invest the time to address and resolve conflict.

There is a reason all the religious and spiritual traditions have practices and rituals. Whether it be yoga, meditation, attending church, prayer, fasting, service or song, they are designed to facilitate the connection between the individual soul and the divine, however and whatever form that takes. But the practice isn't just the time on the mat or in the temple, it's the moment-to-moment awareness and ability to bring that connection into the world, to recognise each other as sparks of the very same divine we may have been honouring or worshipping in the still quiet hours of dawn. In many ways, this is the more difficult practice.

It really boils down to this: that all life is interrelated. We are all caught in an inescapable network of mutuality, tied into a single garment of destiny. Whatever affects one destiny, affects all indirectly.
Martin Luther King Jr

As in society, an organisation is made up of individuals who have one-to-one and one-to-many relationships. The group dynamic as a whole is inseparable from the relationships within it, moulded and shaped by how well its members are able to navigate the treacherous territory of expectations, disappointments, misunderstandings, hazy boundaries of responsibility, unrealistic deadlines and job insecurity. So much is bubbling under the surface, unconsciously playing out in power struggles and ego trips, that the leader's job is often made impossible. To unpick the tangled web of truths and half-truths, stories and bias is like walking a minefield.

And yet, the leader must. To truly be effective and lead a team to greatness requires immense courage, patience and the ability to stay connected – to the individuals and the group as a whole – while simultaneously remaining detached, a cool observer able to perceive what's really going on behind the noise.

The most important thing in communication is to hear what isn't being said.
Peter Drucker

This isn't the place to write a 101 on communication skills, or a summary of conflict resolution techniques. What tends to get overlooked is the necessity to connect and communicate at the level of the heart. Some might say it's not necessary – if you're negotiating next year's budget with your FD or reviewing a contract, what place does the heart have in such activities? But for me, and from the perspective of one who wants to make a difference in the business world, all human connection starts with the premise that at the most basic level we breathe the same air, share a beating heart and, though we may disagree on key topics and have different ideas, we all want to be happy and to know that we are valued and loved. That's the starting point. And when it *is* the starting point – as opposed to an irrelevance that's left outside the door – our attitude towards all business activity shifts. We look for the win–win rather than just what's best for ourselves. We listen more, we take time to explain our position and we are less quick to anger.

When we face problems or disagreements today, we have to arrive at solutions through dialogue. Dialogue is the only appropriate method...
We must work to resolve conflicts in a spirit of reconciliation and always keep in mind the interests of others.
Dalai Lama

Jane Gunn, an expert mediator and author of *How to Beat Bedlam in the Boardroom and Boredom in the Bedroom*, explains it in this way.

At the root of most conflict is dis-connection. It can be viewed quite simply as a crisis or breakdown in interaction that changes the dynamic of the relationship between two or more people. Instead of being open and responsive to each other, people in conflict become closed and self-absorbed.

Imagine two people, Roger and Ed, partners in a small business, who are in conflict with each other. As their conflict develops, their behaviour towards each other is driven by self-protection, defensiveness and suspicion. Mediation helps people in conflict, like Roger and Ed, to shift or move back into their sense of personal strength or self-confidence (Empowerment Shift) and their sense of openness and responsiveness to one another (Recognition Shift). As they do so the interaction can reassume a constructive, connecting and humanising character. They can quite literally reconnect with one another.

So, how can you cultivate positive relationships and channel disagreements into generative conflict? Most how-to guides focus on the external situation and how to deal with it. As always, I like to start from the inside out. Here are a few pointers for you to reflect on and practise the next time you become aware of conflict arising:

- *How conflict averse are you?* Be honest with yourself and if it's something you normally run to the hills to avoid, how can you overcome this so that you're able to deal with it in a timely manner? Coaching is a great support mechanism for this, as is counselling to talk through any childhood-related anxiety around conflict and what it triggers in you.

- *Cultivate curiosity.* If you can develop an interest in how people tick and who they are (underneath the annoying behaviours and habits), then you're halfway there. Being curious means you'll start to observe signs and have insights that otherwise would have eluded you.

- *Be sincere.* George Orwell once said, 'The great enemy of clear language is insincerity.' People will see straight through any attempt to rush to an early solution just to move on; likewise if you try to sweep issues under the carpet. However, when you bring a sincere approach, people will feel safe and able to trust you. In many ways this relates to another spiritual quality, the quality of purity – have a pure heart, and it will help to defuse conflict without even a word being uttered.

- *Let go of the outcome.* As a leader, you may feel your role is to solve the problem, and to drive the situation towards a certain outcome. However, if you see your role as a facilitator, as an objective and detached mediator, then the other parties involved will feel empowered and more bought-in to whatever solution arises.

- *Connect to feelings.* The tendency is to get stuck in the story – the facts and the situation that led to the conflict: 'he said', 'she said'. Listen to the story by all means, but it's difficult to truly resolve conflict and communicate at this level alone. Marshall B. Rosenberg, who developed the Nonviolent Communication system, observed that in the English language we tend to use the words 'I feel' when often we're not connected to our feelings at all. Most people find it difficult to express how they're truly feeling on an emotional level, yet when given an opportunity to express it – in a safe and open environment – they will feel heard, and able to move beyond the 'story'.

The way you speak to others can offer them joy, happiness, self-confidence, hope, trust and enlightenment. Mindful speaking is a deep practice.
Thich Nhat Hanh

Connection is an inseparable part of being human. Group dynamics and conflict in the workplace are common causes of breakdowns that lead to falling productivity and a 'blame culture' that gets in the way of potential being realised. Learning to communicate at the level of the heart is a big part of helping to resolve conflict, allowing all parties to move forward. ◆

1 | Pay attention to how you connect to people you work with – rather than just interacting. Relationships are the lifeblood of an organisation and connection is essential to maintain them.

2 | Dialogue is a skill and practice that leads to open communication – resulting in people feeling 'seen', 'heard' and valued.

3 | Be honest with yourself – look at where your preferences, bias and attachments are getting in the way of connecting with people at a deeper level. Then take steps to prioritise which is most important: maintaining your position or allowing the potential in each relationship to unfold.

◇◇

18

AGILITY – BE THE CHANGE

It is not the strongest of the species that survives, nor the most intelligent…
it is the one most adaptable to change.

CHARLES DARWIN

Angela comes into work one morning and is called into a meeting to hear that her colleague's role is being made redundant and that her role will need to change to incorporate some of her ex-colleague's tasks. Kam discovers on the same day that due to the restructuring process he will no longer be reporting in to his manager of five years, but to a new director recently hired. An entire sales team learn that part of their bonus will now be dependent on the quality of information entered in the new CRM system. At the same time, everyone in the business is aware that there's a due diligence process taking place for a potential acquisition, but nobody's really sure what that means in concrete terms.

A lot has been written on change management in organisations, yet it remains as much of a challenge as ever. There are countless methodologies, processes and programmes – all designed to implement change in the most streamlined, least painful and most effective way possible. By default, people have different levels of tolerance towards change. Yet until each and every individual working in an organisation develops the quality of agility in attitude and behaviour, it will continue to prove problematic.

People don't resist change… they resist being changed!
Peter Senge

Change is often experienced as something that is happening *to* people, rather than a natural process they themselves are a part of, and a partner with. The universe is undergoing change at all times – life itself is a process of continuous creation, sustenance or death. New cells are created in our body on a daily basis, as old cells die and are shed. Memories recede as recent ones replace them. The seasons change, as does our physical response to the external environment. Change is no more than transition occurring on a moment-to-moment basis, and our ability to deal with it is directly linked to our ability to be in flow with it, to explore and dance with it. When I was doing my yoga teacher training, I remember several classes that focused on the transition between the in and out breath, and on the moment where the end of one move would flow into the next. When we draw our attention to the spaces between the action, movement or event, we realise that in effect the whole of life is a series of transitions.

So why is it such a challenge in business? In my opinion it is because people lack this awareness of change as a constant feature of life itself, and lack the experience of engaging with change as a process in their wider lives beyond the workplace. Also, the very word 'change' in the workplace is not usually associated with the smaller, day-to-day shifts in the environment people find themselves in. Change is used for major events – new strategies, initiatives, takeovers, redundancies etc. – events that have a sudden and often unsettling impact on people – largely because they don't feel that they're a partner in the change process. It's being caused by 'them' – usually the executive leadership team, to 'us' – the rest of the company.

Parallels are often drawn between the sports world and that of business. In sports, agility is defined as 'the ability to change the direction of the body in an efficient and effective manner; requiring a combination of balance, speed, strength and co-ordination'. In the business environment, the same definition applies, but needs to be extended beyond the physical body to that of an attitude of mind. When people are able to respond quickly in a balanced way, with leadership strength and resolve, while coordinating existing commitments and priorities, then you have a good recipe for change success. Agility is the proverbial juggling act, and is a key competence for leaders to develop – both at an individual and a collective level. It is the quality that was desperately lacking in Kodak's failure to respond more quickly and effectively to the threat posed by smartphone cameras.

So what can be learned from the field of spirituality in relation to agility and change? Amma often says we need to be like birds sitting on a twig – ready to fly the instant the twig breaks from the tree. It's about being present, while simultaneously maintaining a level of awareness that means we can respond appropriately in the moment. At her ashram in India, in order to foster this practice, there are regular instances where things are changed for apparently no reason in what is otherwise a well-established and routine structure. We are encouraged to develop the quality of being able to detach from 'the' way of doing things, learning to be adaptable in the process. This also develops resilience – another key quality that results from being able to deal with change.

Alex Ferguson is a great example of a leader who embraced agility and change during his reign at Manchester United. He was the first football club manager to recruit and develop youth talent, the first manager to install vitamin D booths, to champion vests with Global Positioning System (GPS) sensors for real-time data and to create a state-of-the-art medical facility to avoid the media hype and publicity when players were admitted to hospital. He said,

> *I believe that you control change by accepting it… Most people with my kind of track record don't look to change. But I always felt I couldn't afford not to change. We had to be successful – there was no other option for me – and I would explore any means of improving.*
> Elberse and Ferguson

The greatest danger in times of turbulence is not the turbulence – it is to act with yesterday's logic.
Peter Drucker

When it comes to organisational agility, there are some key components to foster agility and help manage change:

- *Openness:* Do you have a culture in which anyone and everyone across the company is able to speak up and give critical feedback about a problem or risk to performance? Most leaders I know would nod their heads and say 'Yes, of course.' But really, how do you know? When was the last time somebody did speak up directly? What forums do you have in place to allow feedback and ideas to be fed through to the leadership team? Employee forums, ideas boards, intranet portals and quarterly team reviews asking 'What could we do better?' are all tools that help generate open feedback.

- *Responsiveness:* How quickly can you as a leader respond to feedback from one of your staff or a colleague about concerns in the business? If people see that you are truly responsive to ideas and constructive criticism, and that you take on board what is fed back, you will engender a culture where people feel it is safe to come to you with ideas for change – regardless of whether they are adopted or not (provided you communicate why they are turned down when necessary).

- *Language:* Be clear about what type of language fosters an environment of agility and change, and what language stamps it out. A classic line is, 'We tried that and it didn't work', dismissing an idea or proposal from the start, even if it might be proposed in a different context, and certainly at a different time. Questions such as 'What did we learn from that?', 'What if?...', 'What impact would that have?' all stimulate open and agile thinking about possible change and how to manage it. Gently correct someone who uses language that promotes old or closed thinking and suggest an alternative that could have been used.

- *Modelling:* Gandhi said, 'Be the change you want to see in the world.' It starts with you. If you want to cultivate a culture of openness to change, agility, responsiveness and resilience, you need to model it. Observe how you respond to suggestions in meetings. Become aware of your own natural bias – default modes of judgement that lead you to favour one person's ideas over another's. These are all subtle behaviours that play out at work everyday – the unseen fabric of the organisation. But until you become aware of your own ability to be agile and responsive to change, it will be difficult to lead the way for others.

- *Time:* Ultimately, change takes time. The event itself may take place in the matter of an hour, a day or a week. But the adaptation to change takes longer – the sum total of everyone's individual ability to accept and incorporate the change into their daily lives. It's one of the reasons I dislike the word 'transformation' when used in the context of organi- sational change. At an individual level, events can transform people's lives. But at a collective level, people don't want transformation. Most people want security and safety, and evolution is far less frightening than revolution. Be gentle – if radical change is absolutely necessary, invest the time in ensuring it is as least traumatic as possible. Be realistic about the length of time it will take to see the change in attitude and behav- iour you want to see. Know who your 'early adopters' are and make sure they are not only evangelising the need for change, but supporting others who are finding it a challenge.

I came to the conclusion that the human race is not divided into two opposing camps of good and evil. It is made up of those who are capable of learning and those who are incapable of doing so… learning as the process of absorbing those lessons of life that enable us to increase peace and happiness in our world.
Nobel Peace Prize Winner, Aung San Suu Kyi, on what she learned from six years of house arrest in Burma

Ultimately, in order to realise your own potential as an enlightened business leader, and that of the organisation, you and your teams have to foster an attitude of openness to what's on the horizon, and be willing to learn from mistakes. That's what agility is all about – an attitude of continuous improvement. It's a tricky balance between accepting the present and at the same time keeping one eye to the future, and the potential it holds – recognising that by default what works today might not work tomorrow. It's what I call a 'grounded restlessness' – rooted in the here and now, with the attitude that the here and now could change in the next moment. ◆

◇◇◇◇◇◇◇◇◇◇◇◇◇◇◇◇◇◇◇◇◇◇◇◇ **IN A NUTSHELL** ◇◇◇◇◇◇◇◇◇◇◇◇◇◇◇◇◇◇◇◇◇◇◇◇◇◇◇

1 | Most people experience – and therefore resist – change as an external force over which they have no control. In fact it's an everyday and natural part of life.

2 | In order to cultivate a culture of agility, openness and resilience, you need to 'be the change' yourself. Model the behaviours you want to see in your organisation.

3 | Agility is about being rooted in the present while simultaneously responding to the potential emerging in the future.

◇◇

19

GRACE – CREATE THE RIGHT CONDITIONS

And God is able to make all grace abound to you, so that in all things at
all times, having all that you need, you will abound in every good work.
CORINTHIANS

This, in many ways, is by far the hardest chapter to write… how on earth to write about such a nebulous concept as grace, and how it fits into the concrete, structured world of business? In his excellent book, *What's So Amazing about Grace?*, Philip Yancey writes of a similar dilemma, 'I would rather convey grace than explain it.' But as in most things in life, the fact that it is a challenge shouldn't mean it is pushed aside, in the hope that someone else will provide the answers. Many of the themes in this book require deep reflection to gain insight into how these principles can truly be brought to bear on day-to-day situations in the workplace. If we start from the basis that spirituality is not separate from life itself, then grace is a part of our everyday lives – although we may all relate to it and experience it in very different ways.

So what is grace? Asking the question deep in meditation recently, the answer was very clear: 'Grace is God's expression of infinite love.' How that manifests is multidimensional, manifold, unpredictable and non-discriminatory. The reason we struggle with it is because it is intangible – it doesn't fit the Newtonian view of everything in the universe being fixed according to set rules. But it can usually be recognised in situations where we are surprised by a positive set of circumstances that don't meet our expectations, that don't somehow fit our view of what normal is; when things inexplicably, against all odds, fall into place *exactly* the way they were meant to – in ways we could never have orchestrated ourselves. Believers will often call the evidence of grace a 'miracle', while non-believers will most likely call it 'luck', or 'coincidence'.

At a secular level, grace is part of our everyday language. As Yancey points out, words such as grateful, gratified, congratulated, gracious, gratuity, gratis, ingrate, disgrace and grace period all originate from the word grace. We think of it as a religious term, and yet it is all around us, all the time. Grace is when you overrun on the parking meter yet don't get a ticket. Grace is when you make a huge blunder or oversight at work that could have had serious consequences, but somehow other factors convened and the disaster was averted. Grace is when you apply for your dream role to be told that it's been given to someone else; three months later that person decides to quit and they call you in – at a time when you feel better prepared – psycho-logically and emotionally. Time and again, we experience situations where there are forces beyond our control that have an impact on our day-to-day lives, and we see that our thoughts and actions (our own free will) do not operate in a vacuum, but in a complex web of interdependency with others' actions, fate and an 'invisible force' – called grace.

When I think of the times when grace has flowed through my life, the following occasion comes to me. In 2008 I was working for a small CRM software company. For a long while I had felt like a bird in a cage, desperate to spread my wings and fly. Due to circumstances, I was no longer in an external-facing consulting role, but in an internal marketing role that I found very restrictive. In March that year my husband was rushed to hospital after a minor stroke, and in the course of hospital treatment was diagnosed with suspected lymphoma. On day four of his being in hospital, I was informed that my job would be made redundant due to cost pressures in the business. On the face of it, things were not great. But since I was able to leave work just a few days later, it meant that I was able to spend all the visiting hours available with my husband in hospital, and when he was discharged, the timing and conditions were perfect to set myself up in my own business. I may not have experienced it as grace at the time, but looking back I can see that grace was always present, and that the potential for me to create the life I dreamed of was finally available at that time.

Effort and grace are interdependent;
Without one, the other is impossible.
'Half by humanity, half by God', said the sages.
Effort is humanity's half, and grace is God's.
Amma

If we are to partner with the potential wanting to unfold at any time, then obviously we need to have the right attitude and take action in the right direction, in alignment with our intent and goals. In addition, we need to create the right conditions, and make ourselves as available as possible for the best and highest outcomes.

So how can we make ourselves more available for grace? What if we could create the right conditions for grace to flow through our work lives and business, so that a successful outcome was not just dependent on our own actions and those of others, but somehow magnified by an invisible force? In many ways, just by following all the principles outlined so far, the right conditions will be created. If we demonstrate integrity, serve others through our work, are authentic and mindful and show compassion, we are naturally more available for grace to flow through our lives, and more likely to create the right environment for grace to be present in our day-to-day work.

Additionally, we can look to a definition of grace: 'seemingly effortless beauty or charm of movement, form or proportion'. Beauty is a quality of grace – when we think of something or somebody 'graceful', there is a sense of ease, pleasing to the eye and embodying and bringing to earth the other-worldly, ethereal quality of spirit. Beauty is a quality that I find sadly lacking in the business world. Structures follow straight lines rather than curves, cost considerations demand functional space, and windows and natural light are reserved for the higher echelons. Nature is given a token nod with some flowers at the reception desk and perhaps a few plant pots dotted around. How are we to create the right conditions for grace to flow and manifest if the environment itself fails to mirror the very qualities it is attracted to?

Look at this beauty. There is no reason for what you see.
Experience its grace...
No one, not even Hafiz, can describe with words the Great Mystery.
No one knows in which shell the priceless pearl does hide.
Hafiz

The one striking exception to this that I have seen is Google's offices in London: a 360-degree panoramic view of the city, large floor to ceiling windows that let natural light flood in, outside balconies, and different lounges for rest, reflection and dialogue – including a 'La La Library' in honour of a colleague who passed away, with beautiful furnishings and books spanning every subject.

Another example is of 'living plant walls' that, when combined with other sensory input such as sound and imagery, creates an environment that reflects the purpose of the space. This works well in, say retail, if the aim of that space is to maximise the customer experience of the product or service the retailer is selling.

Of course, not every business has the same level of investment to spend, but it seems that even as a proportion of total revenue, there is a discrepancy between what gets invested in product, systems and infrastructure vis-à-vis the environment staff work in. It doesn't take much – you could invite people who like drawing or painting to bring in their work (or their children's work) to have a temporary exhibition wall space. Works could even be auctioned for charity. Brightly coloured walls, walls dedicated to temporary art and more space dedicated to plants or growing herbs would all help bring grace to the workplace. The potential here is to transform all activity from the purely functional to a higher, more elevated activity that creates connection, enriches the soul and helps to contribute not only to a happier working environment, but the planet also.

I know nothing, except what everyone knows – if there when Grace dances, I should dance.
W.H. Auden

Grace is, by nature, other-worldly, hence it manifests itself in our lives in ways that we don't always recognise or appreciate. Nor do we consider how to make ourselves more available to it, especially in an environment that rewards effort and results and sees only a direct relationship between the two. Since each of us will have a very personal relationship to grace, I offer the following three questions to reflect on, and to assess to what extent you can bring your awareness to how it flows through your life. Allowing grace into your life is a great way to tap into the potential available in every moment.

- What does grace mean to me? How do I define it?
- How do I relate to it? What is my experience of grace on a day-to-day basis?
- How can I make myself more available to receive it, and how can I create the right conditions for grace to flow through my work and business? ◆

1 | Grace is both a personal and an intangible experience, but usually relates to unexpected positive outcomes in a situation (often referred to as luck in secular terms).

2 | In order to allow potential to unfold, we not only have to perform the right actions with the right attitude, but create the right environment and conditions for grace and potential to flourish.

3 | Beauty and nature are physical attributes of grace, which contribute to an environment that supports the realisation of potential.

◇◇

20

VULNERABILITY – BE WILLING TO FAIL

When we were children, we used to think that when we were grown-up we would no longer be vulnerable. But to grow up is to accept vulnerability... To be alive is to be vulnerable.

MADELEINE L'ENGLE

Every time we're put into a new situation with which we are unfamiliar, we make ourselves vulnerable. When we take on a new project, work with different people in the business, apply for a new role, face redundancy, lose a contract or even win a contract, we are vulnerable. We are vulnerable when we are stuck, when we simply don't know what the next step to take is.

How many times have we heard the line, 'Failure is not an option'? At school, we are hardwired early on to associate good results with praise and reward from our parents, equating performance and results with love and acceptance. No wonder we're so afraid of failure. Yet at the same time we are taught to 'learn from our mistakes'. The path of realising our potential is by necessity a learning journey. And every successful entrepreneur will tell you that failure was an important stepping stone on the road to ultimate success – it is inevitable that in reaching for the unchartered territory of unknown potential we'll get some of it 'wrong' along the way.

There is only one thing that makes a dream impossible to achieve: the fear of failure.
Paulo Coelho

On the spiritual level, there is no such thing as failure. Sure, we might slip up every now and then – lose our temper, drink too much or make an excuse rather than extending a helping hand – but ultimately we never fail, it's just that progress might be a little slower as a result. Which helps to take a lot of the pressure off – knowing that, ultimately, as long as your intent is pure and you continue to learn, success will result (albeit perhaps differently from the way you expected). Failure as a concept is literally in the mind – when we think we have failed, it is our bruised ego that is hurting. In a world of perfectionism – air-brushed photos and perfectly polished apples – it can be difficult to accept our own limitations.

Being comfortable with vulnerability is a key part of this process. In Brené Brown's legendary TED talk (see Resources) she speaks of a sense of 'wholeheartedness' that vulnerable people have, a sense of worthiness and a willingness to be truly seen – warts and all. Through years of research she has found that people who live with this sense of 'wholeheartedness' are willing to do something without any guarantees of success, fully comfortable with the lack of certainty of outcome and yet nonetheless willing to step forwards.

Vulnerability is about showing up and being seen. It's tough to do that when we're terrified about what people might see or think.
Brené Brown

It is the fear of failure that holds us back from being our wholehearted selves. And it is this fear that results in us stifling and suffocating our own potential, and that of the teams and organisations we work with. It gets in the way of flow and trust, stunts learning and development and stifles innovation.

I find it interesting that when we take out a pension or look at any investment, an advisor is required to first assess our 'attitude to risk'. We take more time considering risk when considering our financial investment than we do reflecting on our attitude to risk in our lives and business, when the reward is the realisation of our dreams. I'm not talking about the type of risk based on spontaneous and rash actions. Risk can be well thought through and considered, assessed and still deemed to be the right way forward. If failure ensues, there is trust in the collective power of the team or organisation to pick itself up, learn and adjust. Unfortunately, the culture of excess in the financial services industry has led to risk aversion, accompanied by a surge in compliance, regulation and expensive bureaucratic overheads.

Conversely, Google is famous for its 20 per cent policy – where certain departments are allowed 20 per cent of their time to work on any project of their choice, as long as it benefits their customers or the business. On the face of it, this work is risk-free. There are no deadlines to meet, no requirements to satisfy and no personal risk of failure. Out of this 20 per cent emerged Google Earth, Google Maps and Google Mail, and the principle has been adopted by other companies such as LinkedIn's Incubator. They understand that there can be no innovation without risk.

Everything tells me that I am about to make a wrong decision, but making mistakes is just part of life. What does the world want of me? Does it want me to take no risks, to go back to where I came from because I didn't have the courage to say 'yes' to life?
Paulo Coelho

I remember many years ago working for an outsourced training company that worked with global telecoms giants. We provided their sales and technical skills instructors, and at the time had one of the world's best sales trainers – a great guy called Phil. Working in the operations team, I was asked by the client to schedule Phil for a course in a few weeks' time. When I saw that he was booked off that week, I called his boss to ask whether the holiday was flexible – given that this was our largest client and we were negotiating an extended contract with them. The trainer's boss said that no, he wasn't prepared to ask the instructor whether his holiday was flexible. Reflecting on this after the call, I weighed up the pros and cons of calling Phil directly myself. I felt so strongly that it was the right thing to do that I went ahead and, as it turned out, no holiday had been booked or paid for, and he was willing to deliver the course. That decision led in large part to us winning the contract, and although I fast became public enemy number one with his boss, my willingness to take the *right* risk was rewarded and I was offered a relocation package to work on the new project.

The point of this story is that final bit – assessing what is the *right* risk. Are you clear on what the right kind of risk is for your team and your business? Equally importantly – do your team know? Having conversations to explore risks in the context of everyday business is a great way to be open about the grey, fuzzy lines that exist in the business world – and how we feel vulnerable as a result. In a world that prides itself on instant answers from Google Search and Wikipedia knowledge at our fingertips, there are still plenty of nebulous areas where judgement calls are required, and precious little guidance.

Fear of failure and feeling vulnerable also has an impact on our ability to get started on those projects that mean the most to us. Sometimes it is so hard to say 'I don't know', or 'I don't know where to start'. Often, we think we need the whole plan and path laid out before us before we can take the first step. Yet it's only the first step that we need to take – to step out on what we know. It doesn't matter if we don't have the full picture, or know everything we need to know at the beginning of the journey. Take one step. Take one step. Take one step.

Vulnerability is beautiful. Think back to all the times when you have been inexplicably moved to tears. I guarantee that on at least one occasion it was because you saw human-ness laid bare, raw and exposed. That in the willingness to embrace a weakness, there was not a chink of pretence or bravado. If, as an enlightened business leader, you can talk openly about where you take risks in your own life, and reveal your vulnerability, you will create a culture of openness and willingness to let the human side of business shine through, an acceptance that we all bring our strengths and limitations, our emotional baggage and fears, along with all the gifts that they bring. To all of those people working for and with you who are afraid of being judged for who they are, who are afraid of falling down and letting themselves and their colleagues down – give them permission to be their full glorious selves. Frankly, I can think of no greater gift that a leader could give. ◆

Life begins at the end of your comfort zone.
Neale Donald Walsch

◇◇◇◇◇◇◇◇◇◇◇◇◇◇◇◇◇◇◇◇◇◇◇◇◇◇ **IN A NUTSHELL** ◇◇◇◇◇◇◇◇◇◇◇◇◇◇◇◇◇◇◇◇◇◇◇◇◇◇◇◇

1 | We are conditioned from an early age to avoid uncertainty and vulnerability due to fear of failure.

2 | To embrace our vulnerability means embracing our humanity – our imperfections and accepting that while we can never guarantee the outcome of any endeavour we can still 'show up' and give it our all.

3 | Risk aversion doesn't guarantee success, but it does stand in the way of success if it leads to paralysis and too much regulation and bureaucracy. Encourage open dialogue in your organisation and business about the levels of risk that are tolerable in different contexts. Help people to see where it's OK to 'feel the fear and do it anyway', to be comfortable with their own mistakes and vulnerability.

◇◇◇

21

UNITY – DIVERSITY IN ONENESS

*OM. This eternal Word is all: what was, what is and what shall be, and
what beyond is eternity. All is OM.*

THE UPANISHADS

How many organisations have you either worked in or come across
that truly operate as a whole? Where each part knew how its function contributed fully to the whole; where differences were not just tolerated but
appreciated as having a role in ensuring the organisation's success. I can
name a couple that came close, but none that fully managed to live this
ideal day-in, day-out.

Unity is more than alignment. If alignment is ensuring that each function
is in the correct place, carrying out the right work relative to the rest of
the organisation, unity is about functioning as a whole, as a fully integrated,
unified whole. Which is quite a lot to ask – especially as organisations get
larger. What gets in the way?

In my experience, it's because most of us tend to focus more on the
differences, and the lack of cohesion that those differences cause, rather than
operating from the premise that in Oneness there is space for each of us to
express our individual identity, *and* be united. On the one hand we like the
familiarity of working and living with people who share our beliefs, values
and traditions; on the other hand we have a strong separate identity and
sense of being different. Diversity is first and foremost a fundamental part
of life, not just a corporate agenda.

The definition of Oneness according to Google is 'the fact or state of
being unified or whole, though composed of two or more parts'. In the
Eastern tradition there is a time-old metaphor of the ocean and the wave.
The wave is part of the ocean – it has its own life, yet its source is the ocean,

its very essence is the ocean and at the end of its short life it returns to the ocean. So it is with us. We are all individuals with our individual personality, beliefs and ways of seeing the world, and yet we are connected to a greater whole – which could simply be seen as life, and the life force that drives it. In business terms, the wave is each and every business and organisation that supplies its expertise in the shape of products or services and provides employment; the ocean is the wider ecosystem of which it is a part. The two are inseparable. In the same way that the wave and ocean reflect each other (they are both essentially water), the organisation needs to mirror the ecosystem in which it exists – the diversity of the world needs to be reflected in the organisation.

According to the Chartered Institute of Personnel and Development (CIPD) a more diverse workforce brings clear business benefits that go beyond legislative compliance and avoiding litigation costs. It is also:

- Core to people practices to deliver a more engaged and therefore productive workforce;
- A route to fresh thinking, creativity and therefore to market competitiveness and innovation;
- A key element within employer brand management and therefore of strengthening corporate reputation.

But I don't believe we will ever achieve a state of unity by merely managing diversity. I'm not saying that quotas to measure the effectiveness of recruitment drives, talent development and performance management are not necessary. But that's all they should be – measurement tools. Our own internal perspective needs to shift – we need to wear different goggles – because diversity is not just limited to how we relate to people of different race, colour, gender or sexual orientation. In and of itself that is a fundamentally flawed starting point, since it suggests otherness. It's about starting off with the basic premise of all being created equal, of going beyond tolerance to embrace qualities and experiences that others have that are different from our own.

Nor am I saying that more is not needed to create institutions and workplaces that are more accessible and more welcoming of people from different backgrounds; clearly leaders in business have a moral duty to ensure that people of all backgrounds have equal rights and opportunities to work, along with the sense of fulfilment and reward that ensues.

My observation, however, is that something is lost in this process. While the drive for diversity has opened more doors to more people, there is an implicit unspoken message that says, 'Welcome... this is how we do things around here. Conform and you'll be fine.' Which is exactly the point of having a strong culture – the 'way we do things' being the yardstick by which all are judged to fit, or not. But opening doors and recruiting people from diverse backgrounds is not the same as creating an 'inclusive culture' – a culture that allows for multiple perspectives and beliefs to be honoured, listened to and incorporated into business thinking and direction.

Harvard Business Review recently interviewed 24 CEOs of organisations recognised for their diversity. David Thodey, the CEO of Telstra, the Australian telecommunications firm, remarked,

> *In an inclusive culture employees know that, irrespective of gender, race, creed, sexual orientation, and physical ability, they can fulfil their personal objectives by aligning them with the company's, have a rich career, and be valued as an individual. They are valued for how they contribute to the business.*
> Groysberg and Connolly

Sadly, I think too many organisations fall short of this ideal and see the challenge as one of recruitment and retention, rather than seeing the bigger, more holistic picture. I see this in the way women have become incorporated into the workforce. Even the saying, 'women entered the workforce', subliminally reinforces the fact that women did not create the business environment as it exists today. They entered it and had to adapt accordingly. I believe this has had the unfortunate effect of de-feminising women and the business environment. Before I prepare myself to be inundated with a barrage of hate mail, I should elaborate.

We all have masculine and feminine traits, and obviously our gender determines which are most prevalent. Some people have more balanced masculine and feminine traits than others. But in my experience of working with senior level teams and organisations as a whole, the feminine qualities of love, openness, trust, compassion and patience are less prevalent than the corresponding masculine qualities of courage, strength and transactional rather than relational focus. None is more important or valuable than another – on the contrary, we need them all. But I suspect that many women, especially young professionals, subconsciously feel they have to emphasise their masculine qualities in order to fit in and be accepted. This is compounded by an environment that fails to value and allow space for the expression of feminine qualities. This to me means all lose out – men, women and the workplace as a whole.

> *Humanity is divided because man is divided in himself... In the West today the masculine aspect, the rational, the aggressive power of the mind is dominant, while in the East the feminine aspect, the intuitive aspect of the mind prevails. The future of the world depends on the 'marriage' of these two minds, the conscious and the unconscious, the rational and the intuitive, the active and the passive.*
> Bede Griffiths

At the heart of the diversity question is the existential human question of identity. Tolerance, dialogue and respect are critical qualities for a leader and business to develop if they are to truly create organisations that embrace diversity, and ultimately make the final paradigm shift of realising the truth of our Oneness. For a leader and business to reach the highest goal of achieving worthwhile work in the form of profit, purpose, service and legacy, the ability to embrace the paradox of diversity and unity is key.

The new spirituality will produce an experience in human encounters in which we become a living demonstration of the basic spiritual teaching 'We are all one.'
Neale Donald Walsch

◇◇◇◇◇◇◇◇◇◇◇◇◇◇◇◇◇◇◇◇◇◇◇◇◇◇ **IN A NUTSHELL** ◇◇◇◇◇◇◇◇◇◇◇◇◇◇◇◇◇◇◇◇◇◇◇◇◇◇◇◇

1 | Unity can otherwise be termed 'wholeness'. It is the state of being in harmony, and results from the understanding that while each of its parts may be independent, there is a natural interdependence within the bigger whole.

2 | Diversity is so much more than a corporate agenda – it is a natural part of life, and contributes to unity when differences are celebrated and allowed space to express themselves.

3 | Leaders need to create an inclusive culture that mirrors the ecosystem within which the business operates. Tolerance, fairness and appreciation of cultural and gender differences are key aspects of an inclusive culture that allows all stakeholders to thrive.

◇◇

FINAL THOUGHTS

*Sooner or later we admit that we cannot do it all, that whatever our
contribution, the story is much larger and longer than our own, and we are
all in the gift of older stories that we are only now joining.*

DAVID WHYTE, CROSSING THE UNKNOWN SEA

As I hope I've illustrated throughout the book, leadership starts with the
self – with a deep inner connection and profound conviction of your values,
what makes you tick and the behaviours that you need to demonstrate in
order to make a difference to those around you and beyond. Regardless
of your faith or religious beliefs, whether you have them or not, there are
universal principles that when brought to the business world can transform
our own experience of work, and our interactions with others. The result
is not only a more fulfilled and happier workforce, but a more sustainable
business model with less burnout, less turnover, better brand reputation and
a more loyal customer base; one that gives back at least as much as it takes.
In short, an enlightened business.

Several months after writing the preface, I have already seen a further
shift in the conversations I'm having in the business world. Through networking meetings, conferences, and meetings with prospects and clients,
I hear that leaders are all acutely aware of the need to shift from the old
paradigm of how business is run, to a new way of operating. That new way,
which I call enlightened business, is still being defined, and that in a sense
is what makes it so exciting.

Yet while the topic and aims of business as a force for good are now
becoming mainstream – including having a voice at Davos – there is still
much talk about what needs to change and why, but precious little input on
how this change will actually happen. The capitalist model is being revisited,

along with a recognition that long-term change will be difficult as long as businesses are held to account for short-term performance by their investors and shareholders. Research is showing, however, that being a force for good also delivers financial returns that far exceed the average.

In their ground-breaking book *Firms of Endearment*, the authors Raj Sisodia, Jag Sheth and David B. Wolfe share their research into companies who do well by all stakeholder groups – companies who are loved by all who interact with them. These companies consistently outperform the Standard & Poors (S&P) 500 by significant margins. Over five years the Firms of Endearment (FoEs) returned 128 per cent, while the S&P 500 only gained 13 per cent. Interestingly, they have a far greater chance of long-term success (i.e. sustainable) than the companies in Jim Collins' book *Good to Great*. For the authors of *Firms of Endearment*:

To us, a great company is one that makes the world a better place because it exists, not simply a company that outperforms the market by a certain percentage over a certain period of time.

With regards the leadership of these companies, the authors write:

FoEs are bathed in the glow of timeless wisdom. Their 'softness' in a hard world comes not because they are weak or lack courage, but from their leaders' knowledge of the self, psychological maturity, and magnanimity of the soul.

This is why these principles are so important. Because they empower every leader in any organisation to be the change they want to see. While large corporate entities balance long-term survival with short-term firefighting, while movements such as conscious capitalism gain ground and wider acceptance, leaders of any type of organisation can apply ancient spiritual wisdom to their own work and organisation.

People want meaning and purpose in their lives. Presence is now *the* requirement for leaders to have impact, to be heard above the noise. Potential is by definition unlimited – to the extent that we can dream of a world where we are comfortably well off while at the same time enabling others to have the same, we can create it. We are only limited by our own vision and will to take action. In this age of connectivity and collective intelligence, what begins as a movement can quickly become mainstream. We may blame the corporate machine for inertia and being slow to act, but it starts with you and me.

My sincere hope and prayer is that through these chapters you have gained insights into where your own potential lies, tapped into what inspires you and found enough seeds of wisdom to help you take the next step towards creating your own version of enlightened business. Please let me know how you get on – I'd love to hear from you.

BIBLIOGRAPHY/RESOURCES

Barks, Coleman (2001) *The Soul of Rumi: A New Collection of Ecstatic Poems*, New York: HarperCollins

Barrett, Richard (2014) *The Values-Driven Organisation*, New York: Routledge

Benioff, Marc and Southwick, Karen (2004) *Compassionate Capitalism: How Corporations Can Make Doing Good an Integral Part of Doing Well*, Franklin Lakes NJ: Career Press

Binney, George, Wilke, Gerhard and Williams, Colin (2009) *Living Leadership: A Practical Guide for Ordinary Heroes*, Harlow UK: Prentice Hall

Brown, Brené (2012) *Daring Greatly – How the Courage to be Vulnerable Transforms the Way we Live, Love, Parent and Lead*, London: Penguin

Canan, Janine (2004) *Messages from Amma*, Berkeley CA: Celestial Arts

Canfield, Jack (2007) *How to Get from where You Are to Where You Want to Be*, London: HarperElement

Carroll, Lewis (1993) *Alice in Wonderland*, Ware, UK: Wordsworth Editions

Carroll, Michael (2007) *The Mindful Leader: Ten Principles for Bringing out the Best in Ourselves and Others*, Boston MA: Trumpeter Books

Coelho, Paulo (1998) *The Alchemist*, New York: HarperPerennial

Coelho, Paulo (2003) *Eleven Minutes*, London: HarperCollins

Collins, Jim (2001) *Good to Great*, London: Random House Business Books.

Crowe, Thomas Rain (2001) *Drunk on the Wine of the Beloved: 100 Poems of Hafiz*, Boston MA: Shambhala Publications

Dickson, Mike (2010) *Please Take One* - *One Step Towards a More Generous Life*, London: The Generous Press

Einstein, Albert (1972) Letter of 1950, *The New York Times*, 29 March

Elberse, Anita and Ferguson, Alex (2013) 'Ferguson's Formula', *Harvard Business Review*, 1 Oct

George, Bill (2012) 'Mindfulness Helps you Become a Better Leader' *Harvard Business Review*, October, Blog Posts

Gibran, Kahlil (1991) *The Prophet*, London: Pan Books

Gilbert, Daniel and Morse, Gardiner (2012) 'The Science Behind the Smile', *Harvard Business Review*, January

Godin, Seth (2008) *Tribes*, London: Piatkus Books

Griffiths, Bede (1973) *Return to the Centre*, Tucson AZ: Medio Media Publishing

Griffiths, Bede (1990) *The Modern Spirituality Series*, London: Darton, Longman and Todd

Groysberg, Boris and Connolly, Katherine (2013), 'Great Leaders Who Make the Mix Work' *Harvard Business Review*, 1 Sept

Gunn, Jane (2010) *How to Beat Bedlam in the Boardroom and Boredom in the Bedroom*, Evesham: HotHive Books

Harman, Willis W. and Hormann, John (1990) *Creative Work: Constructive Role of Business in a Transforming Society*, Indianapolis IN: Knowledge Systems

Heider, John (1997) *The Tao of Leadership*, Atlanta GA: Humanics New Age

Holden, Robert (2008) *Success Intelligence*, London: Hay House

Howard, Sue and Welbourn, David (2004) *The Spirit at Work Phenomenon*, London: Azure

Johnson, Deborah L., Rev. (2007) *Your Deepest Intent*, Boulder CO: Sounds True

Kofman, Fred (2006) *Conscious Business – How to Build Value through Values*, Boulder CO: Sounds True

Lamont, Georgeanne (2002) *The Spirited Business*, London: Hodder & Stoughton

Langer, Ellen (2014) 'Mindfulness in the Age of Complexity', *Harvard Business Review*, March

Mackey John and Sisodia Raj, (2014) *Conscious Capitalism: Liberating the Heroic Spirit of Business*, Boston MA: Harvard Business School Publishing

Morrish, John (2012) 'Expand your Mindfulness', *Management Today*, June.

Neal, Judi (2006) *Edgewalkers: People and Organisations that Take Risks, Build Bridges and Break New Ground*, Westport CT: Praeger Publishers

Neal, Judi (2012) *Handbook of Faith and Spirituality in the Workplace*

Neal, Judi (2013) *Creating Enlightened Organizations*, New York: Palgrave Macmillan

Neal, Judi and Harpham, Alan (2012) *The Spirit of Project Management*, Farnham: Gower Publishing

Oriah Mountain Dreamer (2003) *The Invitation*, New York: HarperCollins (Element)

Palmarozza, Paul and Rees, Chris (2006) *From Principles to Profit: The Art of Moral Management*, London: Arcturus Publishing

Pink, Daniel (2010) *Drive*, Edinburgh: Canongate Books

Porter, Michael E. and Kramer, Mark R. (2011) 'Creating Shared Value', *Harvard Business Review*, January

Rilke, Maria Rainer (2004) *Letters to a Young Poet*, London: W.W. Norton & Company

Sisodia, Raj, Sheth, Jag and Wolfe, David B. (2007) *Firms of Endearment: How World Class Companies Profit from Passion and Purpose*, New Jersey: Wharton School Publishing

Sri Swami Satchidananda (2000) *The Living Gita: The Complete Bhagavad Gita*, Buckingham VA: Integral Yoga Publications

Steare, Roger (2009) *Ethicability: How to Decide What's Right and Find the Courage to Do it*, GB: Roger Steare Consulting Ltd

Sunley, Jane (2011) *Purple Your People: The Secrets to Inspired, Happy, More Profitable People*, Richmond: Crimson Publishing

The Upanishads (1965) London: Penguin Classics

Thich Naht Hanh (1987) *Being Peace*, Berkeley CA: Parallax Press

Thich Naht Hanh (1995) *Peace is Every Step*, London: Rider Books

Tolle, Eckhart (2005) *The Power of Now*, London: Hodder & Stoughton

Tovey, David (2012) *Principled Selling: How to Win More Business without Selling Your Soul*, London: Kogan Page

Whitmore, John (2009) *Coaching for Performance: Growing Human Potential and Purpose*, London: Nicholas Brealey Publishing

Whyte, David (2002a) *The Heart Aroused: Poetry and the Preservation of the Soul in Corporate America*, New York: Currency Doubleday

Whyte, David (2002b) *Crossing the Unknown Sea: Work as a Pilgrimage of Identity*, New York: Riverhead Books

Wigglesworth, Cindy (2012) *SQ21: The 21 Skills of Spiritual Intelligence*, New York: SelectBooks

Williams, Nick (2011) *Resisting Your Soul: 101 Powerful Tips to Free Your Inspiration*, Brenzett: Balloon View

Yancey, Philip (1997) *What's So Amazing about Grace?*, Grand Rapids MI: Zondervan

Yunus, Muhammad (interviewed by Alison Beard) (2012) 'Life's Work', *Harvard Business Review*, December

All other quotes are from www.brainyquote.com and www.goodreads.com

There are a number of TED talks quoted in the book, including excerpts from Sir Ken Robinson on 'How Schools Kill Creativity' and Elizabeth Gilbert on 'Your Elusive Creative Genius'. I also highly recommend Brené Brown on 'The Power of Vulnerability', and Simon Sinek's 'Start with Why'.

www.amma.org

www.ashridge.org.uk/website/
   IC.nsf/966EA4406D050D388025784C00544774/

$file/MindfulLeadership.pdf

www.b1g1.com

www.Forbes.com/sites/margiewarrell

greatergood.berkeley.edu

www.hrmagazine.co.uk/hro/features/1077271/the-model-csr

netimpact.org/learning-resources/research/what-workers-want

www.psychologytoday.com/blog/prefrontal-nudity/201207/
    smile-powerful-tool

www.slideshare.net/reed2001/culture-1798664, Slide 23

www.tacklementalhealth.org.uk/_assets/documents/
    mental_health_report_2010.pdf

www.valuescentre.com

ABOUT THE AUTHOR

Born in Wales to a Welsh father and French mother, Joolz Lewis has always looked at life from the outside in. Studying languages and spending long periods of time abroad – from Spain to the US to India – reinforced her passion for helping people understand human and cultural dynamics, especially when played out in the workplace.

After the bubble burst on a 5-year stint living the corporate dream in the US, Joolz embarked on an 18-month-long sabbatical that took her from California to the Andes, the Burning Man festival in Nevada and to an ashram in India. Back in the UK her mission has been to inspire and enable business leaders to realise their dreams for personal success while making a difference to others.

Today Joolz coaches and mentors visionary and courageous leaders to connect to their purpose, and to realise their own and others' potential. She also consults with organisations that want to grow in the right way, with universal human values at the heart of their business.

Her philosophy is simple. That deep down, each of us wants to be happy, and that happiness lies in balancing personal success with an innate desire to leave a legacy – big or small. She successfully integrates years of spiritual practice with business experience that is down to earth and practical – integrating heart and mind.

Check out jlew.is/audio to enjoy excerpts from Enlightened Business and commentary read by Joolz Lewis herself as a downloadable MP3.

www.joolzlewis.co.uk
Joolz@joolzlewis.co.uk